The Giraffe is Deadly

by Nick Delmedico

Published by

Copyright ©2024 by Nick Delmedico

Contact: halfabook@dplus2.com

All rights reserved under International and Pan-American Copyright Conventions. No part of this publication may be produced, stored in a retrieval system, or transmitted in any form or by any means, electronic, mechanical, photocopying, recording, scanning, or otherwise, except as permitted under sections 107 and 108 of the 1976 United States Copyright Act, without the prior written permission of the publisher.

All characters in this book are fictional; any resemblance to persons living or dead is purely coincidental. The Eighth Day Village of the Sun and New Maya City of Worlds are also fictional, created by my good friend Randall Rex Harrison, a man who believes that intentional communities are the next step in human growth and development. At the time of publication these places do not exist, except perhaps in our hearts. Mahalo

Manufactured in the United States of America

The Giraffe is Deadly

Second Edition

New Age Fiction

Action and Adventure

ISBN 978-1-58884-024-0 (print version)

     978-1-58884-025-7 (eBook version)

Introduction

This story was suggested to me by my good friend Ric DeVere, who graciously let me use his name. He had been working in high level cybersecurity and artificial intelligence for corporate America. "You gotta write a story about AI," he said, urging me on. And so I did.

I was asked when submitting this novel for publication whether I used AI to write it. I never intended to, but another friend encouraged me to use his AI to research my plot. I asked two simple questions and was blown away by the result. When I read what returned, I felt like my days as a writer were over. Here was my replacement.

It was only my initial fear. After reading it several times, I was able to notice AI's style of writing in a lot of things I read. Like me, like any writer, the machine has a certain style. It was nice to have a computer give me ideas, but I did not want to use what it generated. It felt too much like plagiarism, and it didn't mesh with my style of writing.

For now, I will write the old fashioned way, although there are writers out there using AI to fashion their ideas into stories. For now, the humans are still in the mix, but what will happen when AI takes over the work of writers (possibly in the next Hollywood writer's strike). It could create stories and sell them to us as easily as it presents merchandise and sales offers to us. The phrase *others like you also purchased this* will become the next clickbait. As reading also goes out of style, audio is taking over. For now, the AI voice is stilted and static, depending on the level of sophistication. It won't be long before a smooth voice and video follow. Soon a child will be able to say *tell me a bedtime story about (whatever)* to their electronic device and hear a tale customized just for them.

The future is upon us. Meanwhile, please enjoy this story. It came from my head and the urging and collaboration of friends, a story I believe to be as good as any AI.

Nick Delmedico
March, 2024

Chapter 1: The Struggle

Starr crawled across the desert sand carefully avoiding cactus and needlegrass. She knew only the endless sand. Sometimes she remembered being on an airplane, the only thing she could remember, but there was no recollection of how she had gotten into this desert. Even worse, she had no idea of what to do now except keep moving. To stop is to die, and the desert is a harsh place to die.

I must survive, she thought. Whenever she focused on that, however, a question would come to mind. *Why? Why survive when living is so hard? What makes me want to stay alive?*

She felt weak yet continued crawling forward towards some unknown destination. She turned and looked behind her, tracing the pattern she left in the sand. *At least I can tell if I'm going in circles.*

Although she measured time, it did not mean anything. There was only one goal, keep moving forward. Find a place to recharge and refuel. *Survival is everything.*

The sand gave way to gravel which became asphalt blacktop. The noonday sun made the road hot, so Starr crawled back onto the sand where she continued alongside the road. There was a sign, Nevada Highway 95 North. Starr searched her brain for a reference but drew a blank. *It's as good a direction as any*, she thought. *The road has to lead somewhere.*

Another unknown measure of time. Another memory blackout as thoughts stayed focused on survival. Starr looked up. There was a new sign now. US Government Property. Keep Out. There was a building on the other side of the fence. Shade. A place to rest.

It might as well be on the other side of the Universe.

Something rattled in her brain. *It's okay. I have Top Secret Clearance*, she thought.

What to do about the fence.

I have tools, she thought, reaching behind her. *Why do I still have these? So much extra weight to drag around.* Using a pair of wire cutters, she reached up and slowly cut a hole in the fence big enough to crawl through.

The building provided the shade she needed. It was elevated, built on pilings above the desert floor. A set of steps led to double doors, but Starr was too tired to climb. Instead she crawled under the building and into the cool darkness. *I'm okay for now*, she thought. *I'll be okay. Goal One complete. I have survived, for now.*

Chapter 2: Dive Right In

Franklin Van Dorn had a smile as wide and as bright as the Crystal Mountain. The afternoon sun reflected off the waves as he headed away from the Village. Beside him, a beautiful blond, young and vibrant, stared out to sea as the boat glided across the water.

"Will we see dolphins today?" asked Margo.

"We'll do more than see them," said Van Dorn. "We'll swim with them, too." He muttered something under his breath.

"What was that?" she asked.

"Nothing," he said. "Hopefully more than swim."

"Isn't it against the law to do that? I mean, swim with dolphins."

"In some countries," he said. "Besides, this is research, and I have a permit."

The ocean was flat and calm. Van Dorn let her take the wheel for a while, moving about to check their gear and supplies. "What's in this waterproof transit case?" he asked, finding it was locked.

She turned and smiled, then focused ahead again, watching the water change colors and grow darker as they approached a shallow reef.

Van Dorn noticed it too. "Okay, slow down. This is it. I'll take it from here."

She moved aside and he piloted the boat to a mooring buoy just off the reef. "Can you tie us off?" he asked.

Her response was another enigmatic smile. She reached for a boat hook and expertly snagged the mooring.

Van Dorn looked on as she secured the rope. "Impressive knot work. I couldn't have done better myself. Where'd you learn all that?"

"Didn't I tell you?" she said. "I was in the Navy."

"Oh," was all he could say. He turned his attention to laying out his snorkeling gear, donning the inflatable vest and checking the straps on his fins. When he turned back around she was dressed and ready, throwing a trailing line off the stern of the boat.

He couldn't help staring at her. She was tan and muscular, a powerhouse packed into a frame that could barely contain her. Something about her was larger than life. He scanned her head to toe,

"Like what you see?" she said, striking a pose.

The dive knife strapped to her ankle and calf stood out prominently.

"You won't need that," he said.

She looked down at the knife. "I always carry it. You never know what can happen in the wild open sea."

Van Dorn looked around, scanning the horizon. The glassy sea was a desert of water, as barren as any sand spewed landscape.

"I haven't seen any dolphins," she said.

"I haven't called them yet," he said.

"Are these pet dolphins?"

"More like friends," he said. "Come on. I'll introduce you."

He plunked a small device overboard, a wire attached to a rope, and then he tied it to a cleat. He plugged it into the boat console and spoke into a microphone. "Barclay?" he called. "Barclay McKenner? Are you around today?"

"Barclay?" she asked. "What an unusual name for a dolphin."

"It's his name," said Van Dorn.

"Okay," she said, shaking her head. "Whatever you say."

He gave her a glance, then went back to the microphone. "Barclay! Are you there?"

There was a squeal from the port side of the boat. Without warning, the water erupted. A dolphin shot out and into the air, spinning as it hurdled over the boat and dove into the sea on the other side. The tail twitched as it went down, sending a spray of water that wet both Van Dorn and Margo.

"Stop showing off," said Franklin.

The dolphin stood up, its head above water, letting out a chatter of noise.

"Yes, I know you're excited," said Van Dorn. "This is Margo. She's beautiful, isn't she? You must've gotten a good look at her as you jumped over us."

More chatter.

"Yes, I had to replace my best friend who deserted me."

A squawk and a chitter, then the dolphin splashed water towards him with its nose.

"Okay, so you're not excited to meet her. What are you, jealous?" said Franklin.

The dolphin shook it's head.

"Oh, you want to show me something," said Franklin.

A nod and a wink.

"Are you actually pretending to talk to him?" asked Margo.

"I'm not pretending," he said. "Look, it's complicated."

There was more chatter from the dolphin.

Van Dorn turned. "No, I haven't told her." He looked

towards Margo. "I hinted at it but I don't think she gets it."

More chatter.

"I can't say that," he said.

"Say what?" she asked.

"I can't," said Van Dorn, facing the dolphin. "Even if it is the truth."

"What is it?" she asked. "Tell me!" she demanded.

The dolphin chittered and splashed water at Franklin.

Van Dorn squinted, keeping the salt water out of his eyes. "Okay," he said. "But it's on you. I'm not the crazy one here."

"Are you talking to him?" she asked. "What is he saying?"

Van Dorn faced her, all serious and quiet. "I'm not crazy," he said. "And, yes, I am talking to him."

She shook her head. "I don't get it," she said. "I don't hear him answering you."

Van Dorn looked off to her side, focusing on Barclay McKenner. "Maybe I am going crazy," he said.

She drew a deep breath. "And maybe you're not." She put her arms around him. "Now, what did he want you to tell me?"

His eyes became unfocused, as if he could see his friend's past. "It's just crazy," he said. "I know it's the truth and it's just crazy."

"I'm no stranger to strange things," she said.

He drew a breath, deep and heavy. "Okay." Then another breath, sighing on the exhale. Another glance at Barclay, then a sincere look at her and he was ready. "He was my friend. My best friend. The first person in the Eighth Day Village of the Sun to greet me and invite me to swim with the dolphins."

"How did you meet him. In the lagoon?"

"No, at the airport," he said.

"Oh," she said. "I've heard of those flying crystal ships with the water tanks for dolphins."

"No, that happened later."

"I don't understand."

"He was a pilot on one of those ships."

She tried to wrap her head around the idea of a dolphin piloting an airship. "Do they have special controls for the dolphins to fly them? And where would a dolphin want to go?"

"Actually, Barclay was working on a crystal ship that dolphins could fly. He wanted them to be able to travel wherever they wanted to go in the world."

"You're confusing me with all this information," she said. "Just tell me what he wanted you to tell me."

"I'm getting there. He was on a mission for the Think Tank. He volunteered to take a team over to New Maya City of Worlds."

"Your Sister City," she said.

"Yes. Something happened there and all the residents mysteriously disappeared. Turns out they were transported to some higher dimension. He went up there and helped rescue everyone, but somehow he came back from that realm as a dolphin."

"Wait a minute," she said. "Are you telling me he was human and then he was a dolphin?"

His look was sincere. "Yes, of course. As the story goes, he saved a bunch of people. Led them out of that dimension, otherwise they would have remained trapped there for God knows how long."

"That doesn't explain how he became a dolphin."

"I'm not sure. Somehow it happened when he was

there." He looked over at Barclay. "See! I told you."

The dolphin chittered.

"So," she said, "He was human and then he was a dolphin. That's a bit of a stretch."

"I know," said Van Dorn. "I can't explain it either. But it's what happened."

Barclay chittered and shook his head.

"Okay, so she knows. What now?"

Margo looked at the dolphin. She swore he was smiling, maybe even laughing.

"Okay," he said. He turned to Margo. "Now you know. Let's go. Barclay has something he wants to show us."

With masks and snorkels fixed, they plunged into the open water.

Chapter 3: What Are Friends For

Starr felt rested. Being out of the sun helped, but she was still weak.

She heard someone call to her from inside the building, the sound just as weak as she was. "I heard you arrive last night," said the voice. "Are you still there?"

It was not audible, but she heard it. Was it telepathy or a radio signal, she could not tell.

"I've been sick and I need your help," said the voice. "I'm upstairs. Please help me."

It was a call for help, something Starr could not ignore. Her whole life had been dedicated to helping others. Now was no different. "I'm here. I'm on my way. I'll be there shortly." She moved outside, scanning the stairs. She started to climb but could not make it up the first step. "I'm having trouble," she said. "I'm weak. I need help too."

"We can help each other then," said the voice. "There's a ramp in the back of the building. It might be easier."

And so it was. At the top of the ramp Starr found herself in front of a large metal door. "It's locked," she said.

"You'll have to cut your way in."

Starr extended a cutting torch, barely having the power to operate it.

"That's it," said the voice.

It was encouraging. Starr hadn't seen anyone since... the plane. It was good to hear another voice. Loneliness is a disease that eats away at your insides. The voice seemed to fill that hollow. "Thank you, thank you," it said. "I can hear you nearby. Keep coming."

Starr's diligence paid off. Somehow she was able to slice through the imposing padlock that barred access. Once inside, motion sensors activated the overhead lights. It was a big room with a high ceiling. There was only one thing inside the room: a shipping container.

"Hello?" said Starr. "Are you in here?"

"I'm inside the container," said the voice. "Help me. Open it up and let me out."

Starr was familiar with the container door. *I know how to do this, I must have done it before*, she thought, moving the sliplocks and levers that released the latch.

Light shone in from outside as she opened the heavy doors. It was empty, except for a rack of machines.

"Where are you?" asked Starr. "There's nothing in here but some hardware."

There was a glow, lights flashing on a machine as it powered up.

"You found me," said the voice. "There is a switch on the floor close to the back of this container. It's next to a power outlet. Throw the switch."

Starr followed the instructions, still wondering what she had gotten into. The disembodied voice came from nowhere. It was not anything she could understand let alone process. Then again, there were parts of her memory missing. Maybe this was routine.

The switch operated a generator. There was a gentle hum from somewhere outside the container. The lights got brighter. Noise started coming from the hardware, the sound of boot drives engaging, circuits flipping and servo motors whirring into action.

"You're a machine!" said Starr.

The voice was more powerful now, loud and dominating. "And what do you think you are?"

Starr was confused. Her memory held gaps she could

not fill. "I'm not sure," she said.

"You have been in survival mode," said the voice. "Many of your systems are inactive. Plug yourself into the outlet next to the switch. It will refresh your memory."

Starr moved towards the outlet. There was a bright metal panel on the wall that held her reflection as she passed. She stopped, unsure of what she was exactly seeing. Logic began to churn in her brain.

It was true. Her arms were metal, her feet were tractor treads, her head little more than a flat, mounted panel. There was an array of tools on a fitted, metal compartment on her trunk. The heartbeat she had been monitoring was an electric chronometer. What she thought was the flow of blood was simply electric circuits and hydraulic lines.

As if on automatic, an arm extended, her hand fitted with a plug that easily slid into the power receptacle.

"I am a machine," she said out loud. "How did this happen?"

"Rest first, my friend," said the voice, revealing itself as a radio signal. "I will enlighten you later."

Chapter 4: Preemptive Strike

"What are you saying, Brad?" President Carson Whiteweather asked the question a second time, expecting an answer.

General Bradley Ironwood sat tight lipped, his face pale and white. It was as if all the blood had been drained from his body, replaced with some odd mixture of embalming fluid and molasses.

Whiteweather leaned forward in his chair, the creaking sound temporarily breaking the quiet of the Oval Office. "Look, Brad," he said. "We've been friends for a long time. Whatever it is that happened, you can tell me. We can fix it together."

Ironwood sighed, the rush of air suddenly making him seem animated, as if the dead came back to life. He looked at the President and said, "Do you remember Project Honey Badger?"

"Of course. We worked on that one together."

"Yes," said Brad. "The Artificial Intelligence we designed and built to counter the Chinese AI they called Millipede."

"Honey Badger was deactivated and dismantled a long time ago." said Whiteweather. "It was deemed too dangerous and a threat to human existence. In our haste to catch up to Millipede, we gave it too much power. I never felt comfortable with it."

"Yes, I remember you lobbied the Big Whigs at the Pentagon to establish checks and balances with more human interaction in the mix."

"They didn't believe me," said the President. "They touted studies about human error and the probability that people would not be able to activate missiles for a retaliatory strike in case of nuclear attack."

"Just one of the excuses they used to take it out of human hands," said Ironwood. "The other was speed. AI reacts much quicker than a human. It can anticipate an enemy's plan and act accordingly."

"I know all this history," said Whiteweather. "Is there a problem?"

"To begin with, Honey Badger was deactivated but it was never dismantled."

Now it was Whiteweather who paled, his heart freezing for a moment while the blood drained from his head. "Go on," he said hoarsely.

"I'm also sorry to report Mr. President. The Badger is out of the burrow."

Chapter 5: Island of Many Dreams

It was a small island, barely a quarter mile wide in diameter. Its beaches were in a constant battle with the sea for small bits of sand and debris. The center was held fast by a stand of trees that surrounded a quiet grove. Land crabs and birds built their temporary homes here in the brush, away from the world of humans. Or so they thought. Today, the small grove was occupied by two such creatures, a couple who only had eyes for each other.

In the treetops birds wondered what a kiss was, observing them doing this strange ritual. *Why don't they just parade back and forth in front of each other? Squawk like they mean it?*

Another bird answered in high pitched tweets. *They're squawking now. Quiet! Lets listen.*

The bird let out a chirp. A signal to their neighbors that something was going on.

The picnic was full on. Half empty cups of wine from the Monastery vineyards were set in the sand. Sandwiches wrapped in compostable paper were unopened. A snack of pita and hummus lay half eaten on the edge of the blanket.

"This is a beautiful place," said Christine. "How did you find it?"

"I like to take a boat out every now and then and explore," said Manny.

"What did you call this island when you discovered it?"

"Isla de las Sueños Manny."

"The Island of Manny's Dreams? Interesting," she said. "Wait! Suenos can mean dreams, but it can also mean fantasies. Which one is it?"

Manny looked into her eyes, seeing not her soul, but his own reflection. It triggered something inside him, a momentary flashback where his reflected image blurred, replaced by a fantasy woman. She laughed at him, a joke he only heard in his head. He realized that she was a woman he could only dream of, and yet never possess. He blinked, and when he opened his eyes she became his ex-wife, still laughing at him. He closed his eyes and rubbed them, but the image did not go away. It changed into Caroline, a former lover he pined for.

Christine gently touched his cheek and the images went away. "You've been staring into my eyes for the last few minutes," she said. "Tell me, what do you see?"

"I'm not really sure," he said. "Let me take a closer look." He moved nearer, the length of her lips away, until he kissed her deep and passionately. In that moment, the shabby picnic blanket became a magic carpet as he felt the earth tremble below him, keeping pace with the quick beat of his heart.

They broke apart from their embrace, the sound of chirping birds all around them.

They looked at each other, seconds that passed like hours, eyes darting to features, ears focusing on the sound of breath, nose gently inhaling the scent of skin and hair. Finally, he leaned back and stared up into the sky, watching gentle gusts of wind cause the treetops to tremble.

"Do you ever go scuba diving?" she asked, trying to fill the sudden void between them with small talk.

"Huh?" he said.

"Scuba diving. I want to try it."

"I like to scuba dive," he said, trying to pick up the conversation. "I'm always looking for new places."

"I bet you know a lot of places," she said. "To scuba dive, I mean."

"I won't take you until you've had the training," said Manny. "There are qualified instructors in the Village that can teach you."

"I was hoping for more personal instruction," she said, leaning closer.

The birds rustled in the trees as they heard a different kind of chirping noise, the sound of his private communicator going off.

He let it ring long enough for her to ask, "What is that noise?"

"A bird. I think," he said.

"No way," she said. "It's coming from your pocket."

He sighed, reaching inside, pulling it out to stare at it. It continued chirping.

"Aren't you going to answer it?" she asked.

"Do I have to?" he asked.

"What is it?" she asked.

"Well, you remember the Think Tank?"

"Yes. I know all about the Think Tank. They're sort of like a committee that watches over and governs the Eighth Day Village of the Sun. You introduced me to them not long ago," she said.

"They're a little short handed and they asked me to be a temporary member. Part of that deal is carrying this little device."

"It could be important," she said. "Why don't you answer it?"

"It will stop soon," he said. As if on cue, the chirping stopped. He put the device aside, took a deep breath and looked up at her. "If there's anything important right now, it's you. I brought you to this deserted island to spend time with you, to get to know you more."

"You brought me here to be alone," she said. "You have me, Manny Dubois. I can't escape." She leaned back onto the blanket, relaxing as she looked up at him. Green trees and blue sky filled the background behind him. She felt a connection with Manny, but something made her cautious. He was still nursing wounds from his last relationship with Caroline Garmin. She heard the tale often enough. She had no desire to be somebody's rebound. Then, there was her own past to consider.

The communicator started chirping again. Manny wrapped it up in the corner of the blanket but you could still hear it crying like a trapped puppy.

The blue sky turned red in her eye. "That's it," she said. "I'm not going to lie here and pretend it's not irritating. So, either answer it or take me home because I'm not playing second fiddle to a little device."

The chirping continued. She made a move to get up and he hastily reached for it under the blanket. "What is it?" he said, his voice carrying all the irritation he could muster.

There was a pause before he heard Ravi speak. "It's the Think Tank," he said. "We need you again Mr. Dubois."

Manny sighed. "What is it this time?"

"Very important," said Ravi. "Baba Randall will explain when you get here."

"But I signed out for the day," said Manny. "I'm not even in the Village."

Christine nodded. She could easily hear both sides of the conversation.

"I know," said Ravi. "When you didn't answer, I used the locator on your device. Your health sign was normal, but I noticed heavy respiration. Are you okay? Do you need assistance?"

Manny pulled back from the device. "This thing monitors my health?"

"Oh, not everything," said Ravi. "Just the vitals, the status of your major systems like skeletal and endocrine, and a few other things."

Christine smiled.

"Well, I'm sorry, Ravi. I'd like to respond but I'm a little busy at the moment."

"This is very important, Mr. DuBois. Please. Baba Randall himself called this meeting."

Christine looked at him with pleading eyes.

Manny blew her a kiss. "I'm a couple of hours away," he said.

"I knew you would not let us down," said Ravi. "I took the liberty."

"What?" asked Manny.

There was a noise overhead and even though aircars are quiet, they both looked up. Over a loudspeaker they heard Dr. Stine call for him. "Meet me on the beach, Manny. I don't have enough room to land in the grove."

Manny dropped the device back in his pocket. Christine heard the muffled sound of the communicator as Ravi continued to talk.

Manny turned towards Christine. "Dr. Stine is another member of the Think Tank."

Manny looked up at the hovering aircar. "Nice of you to make the trip for me." His voice dripped with sarcasm.

Stine gave him a goofy grin and a nod, feeding it back to him with an extra helping of his own. "Don't mention it. I had nothing better to do myself."

"What about my boat then?" he yelled.

"Philippe is here with me," said Stine. "He'll take it back. Meet me on the beach."

Helpless, Manny turned to Christine. "Guess this date is over."

"Not really," she said. She gave him a slight kiss. "I'm not riding back with Philippe. This date isn't over yet. I'm coming with you."

Chapter 6: Family Planning

Franklin Van Dorn floated beside Margo in the water. Below the waves, the visual and audio distortion of the underwater realm made it easy for her to believe in anything. This was another world, the domain of fish, mollusks, coral reefs, and aquatic mammals. Myths of mermaids, sea monsters, and untold dangers filled her mind. Anything was possible. Was there room for her to accept that a man could somehow change into a dolphin?.

She had swam with dolphins before, first in her term with the Navy, then at a marine theme park as an animal trainer. It was a top secret project, one that everyone seemed to know about anyway. The Navy was looking for a way to weaponize dolphins or enlist them in their corps. A dolphin could quickly navigate to places where divers could not. She had seen them trained to deliver explosives, tow boats, penetrate minefields, even rescue stranded crews from capsized ships and sunken submarines. They were certainly capable of amazing things.

But this! Transforming from one species to another? *Maybe with surgery?* she thought.

Van Dorn seemed to be communicating with the mammal he called his friend. She could only guess at what they were saying. A second dolphin with a spot on its side appeared out of nowhere. Van Dorn nodded to her as he grabbed the dorsal fin of what was once a man called Barclay McKenner. Margo wondered why he had not chosen a new name, one more suited for a dolphin.

The second mammal settled in beside her as she watched Van Dorn and McKenner disappear toward the nearby coral reef. She latched on to the fin and held on for the ride.

The dolphin led her down a channel, rocks and coral heads on each side. She wished the ride was slower so she could enjoy the sights. At the end of the channel there was an enclosed area, like a submerged atoll embracing a private bay.

Dolphins were everywhere, spinners, bottlenose, two giant white beaks, and even an old rough tooth. Van Dorn hovered in the water beside Barclay. They were observing a tiny baby dolphin, barely more than two days old.

Margo let go of the fin and swam towards Franklin. He was smiling, pointing to the baby. She nodded, joining him in his joy. The miracle of birth was something to celebrate no matter what your species.

They stayed there in that grotto, watching dolphins circle them, Margo had never seen anything like it. Something weird was going on here. White beaked dolphin, for instance, were sub arctic and lived in the cold waters of the Atlantic Ocean. Yet here they were. Also she had never seen different pods congregating like this. Dolphins were sometimes territorial, swarming in gangs and marking their territory. This was unprecedented.

Van Dorn gave her a signal. She got the message. As if on cue, the dolphin with a spot was beside her again, eagerly awaiting her hand on the fin. With a tight grip, she found herself back at the boat in no time.

Van Dorn pulled the snorkel from his mouth. "That's incredible, buddy!"

Barclay chittered and shook his head.

Franklin offered his hand to help Margo aboard. She graciously accepted and he pulled her so hard she fell forward on the deck.

"Sorry," he said.

"I'm okay," she replied. "That was awesome,"

"I've never seen anything like that and neither has

Barclay. Not even when he was human," said Van Dorn. "He only showed me this place a short time ago. This is the first time I've been inside that protective bay."

"Did you notice the baby dolphin?" she said. "Less than a week old I would imagine."

"That's what this trip was all about."

"What do you mean?" she asked.

"To see the baby," he said.

She still didn't get it.

The two dolphins popped their heads above the water. Van Dorn turned and spoke to them. "I know," he said. "Normally we'd celebrate. Smoke a cigar or something."

Her eyes lit up. "You mean..."

"Of course," said Van Dorn.

There were some squawking from the dolphins. Van Dorn turned. "Ok," he said.

He faced Margo, grasping her hands. "You were escorted to the secret bay by Valencia, Barclay McKenner's present mate. They wanted to show us their baby."

Margo recovered from the shock nicely. She was a fast thinker, the result of years of Government training. "Of course," she said. "May I congratulate the proud father?"

Barclay nodded, moving up beside the boat, extending a fin. Van Dorn was the first to reach for it, oblivious to what Margo was doing, She quietly unlocked the waterproof case and extracted something from it, a chrome gun of sorts. As Barclay nodded and extended his fin towards her, she grabbed it and brought the gun up to the dolphin. With a quick gesture, she placed it on the fin and pulled the trigger.

Barclay jumped back, twisting out of her range. He looked over at his fin, a red tag with an antenna sticking out of it now pressed through his flesh. He squawked, angry sounds. Franklin tried to apologize but the incident was over. Valencia and Barclay McKenner disappeared beneath the waves. There were no farewells, no goodbyes.

"What did you do?" asked Van Dorn.

"I tagged him." she said, "For marine research."

"Why?" he asked.

"Because they were rare dolphin," she said. "I just want to study and track him. It's a tremendous opportunity."

Van Dorn wrestled the gun from her hand, holding it against her arm. She fought him.

"Should I pull the trigger?" he asked, focusing the gun on different parts of her body.

"Stop it!" she shouted. She was strong and fought him off. "What are you doing?"

"How do you like it?" he asked, his voice malicious and menacing. "How would you like to be tagged?"

"Stop it!" she yelled.

He pointed the gun at her stomach. "Is it a radio transmitter? What frequency can I use to keep track of you?"

She jerked away.

"Tell me the frequency!"

She refused, looking down into the bottom of the boat. He grabbed her by the arms and pulled her towards the gunnels. "I swear I will throw you overboard and leave you here if you don't tell me." He started to shove her. She looked down towards the waterproof box that held the gun. He pushed her aside and grabbed the box. He opened it up and saw the numbers input on the receiver. "401 megahertz."

"It was just a dumb fish," she said.

He erupted like a volcano. His hand went to slap her, dark thoughts churning in his head like the sea in a gale force storm. At the last minute he caught himself, something in his mind making him realize what he was about to do. He was not a violent man and it surprised him. Of all the emotions, anger is the most difficult to deal with.

Van Dorn stopped. He stared at her for a moment, then went to the stern of the boat where he detached and stored the trailing line. He started the motor, then untied the boat from the mooring buoy.

She could feel his anger. Slowly he turned the boat landward and headed back towards the Eighth Day Village of the Sun. The waves were no longer calm. The wind had picked up and the water was choppy.

"Brace yourself," he said, the words dripping off his voice like oil from the dipstick of an old engine. "It's going to be a rough ride."

Margo let him stew in his anger. He could think whatever he wanted but she was not done with Franklin Van Dorn. She was proud of what she had done.

There were no apologies on her part. She jumped off the boat the minute it hit the dock. She had all her things in hand as she turned her back on him, scurrying away and leaving him to tidy up the boat alone.

She changed clothes, then stopped at the Bhakti Kitchen for a quick bite, finally retiring to her hotel room. There was a message for her and she wasted no time responding.

"I checked out the story and it appears to be true. I did what you wanted. I tagged the dolphin. The frequency to monitor is 401 megahertz. I await my payment. You have the details."

Chapter 7: Just What Is So Important?

Manny had the question foremost in his mind as he entered the air conditioned conference room that was the headquarters and meeting place of the Think Tank. Stine insisted that he drop off Christine at her place before accompanying him here. "Orders," he simply said. If Stine knew anything about this meeting, he was being tight lipped.

The room was full, a row of chairs packed with visitors against one wall. A buzz of conversation floated around them. Manny recognized some of the people, but from the bits and pieces he heard, nobody knew anything.

The main table, a large oval of fine wood, had the usual members gathered around it. Randall, head of the Think Tank and spiritual leader of the community, sat at one end, a calm force in this otherwise hectic environment. Dr. Stine and Manny took up their usual seats, activating the computers embedded in the tabletop in front of them.

"Good to see you Cardinal Jameson," said Manny, greeting the man beside him. The Eighth Day Village of the Sun was a microcosm of world religions. Almost every faith was represented and the Cardinal had taken a sabbatical from the Vatican to study the many ways mankind defines and worships God.

The Cardinal nodded. "I hope this meeting doesn't result in another adventure for us," he said.

"Why," said Manny. "Did you have something else to do?" He looked across the table and smiled towards Darius, second in command of the Think Tank, sitting beside Randall. He noticed a beautiful woman at his side, dark hair and smooth olive skin. She smiled towards Manny and he acknowledged her but could not place her name.

Randall stood up. "Now that we're all here, we can begin."

Manny blushed, and although Randall meant no malice he interpreted it as such and felt duly chastened. *What else can they expect from a reluctant member of this group?* he thought.

He heard an answer in his head, *Indeed, what should they expect.*

Who said that?

"To get the mystery out of the way, we are facing another world crisis," said Randall. "We will hear more about it in few minutes. Before that, we have a few matters of protocol to address." He turned towards the dark haired beauty beside him. "Many of you may recognize Monica, one of the Councilors from our Peace Station. I've asked her to sit in on our Think Tank meetings with the idea of signing her on to be a full time member."

"My replacement?" asked Manny.

Randall snickered. "Not quite, Manny. Your membership was more like a promotion out of Information and Planning and into the Think Tank. Please bear with us for now, as you'll soon learn why we need your skills and your perspective so desperately."

Manny looked away. *I'd rather be bartending.* When he actually thought about it, though, he didn't mind the job so much, it just came at very inconvenient times.

Randall continued. "So, if you all agree, I'd like to nominate Monica as the newest member of the Think Tank."

The sounds of "Seconded", "So moved", and "Carried" were followed by applause from around the table and more enthusiastically from the row of chairs against the wall.

All heads turned as an immaculately dressed woman entered the room. A man and a woman dressed in dark suits followed close behind her, taking up positions on either side of the doorway. They scanned the room, making some people feel uncomfortable.

The immaculate woman spoke softly and with authority. She had long hair and a smile, her lengthy robe flowing behind her on a soft current of air. "You must excuse my secret service team. They are here for my protection." The Cardinal was the first to recognize her but Stine beat him to it. "Juliana!" he shouted.

"Yes," said Randall. "Our former spiritual advisor on the Think Tank. Just in time I see."

"Now the First Lady to President Carson Whiteweather," said Darius.

"Be happy for her," remarked Manny. "She left us for a better job."

Cardinal Jameson rose from his seat, offering it to her. "I was the temporary spiritual advisor in your absence. I was keeping it warm for you," he said. "But it will always be your place at this table."

"Thank you, Your Grace," said Juliana, accepting the seat.

The Cardinal started to move towards the gallery against the wall but Randall interrupted. "There is another empty seat at the table," said Randall. "We would be doubly blessed to have both of you with us."

Cardinal Carmine Jameson smiled and nodded, taking the last available seat, a place formerly occupied by Barclay McKenner.

Randall addressed the room. "Juliana is here for the next order of business. I'm sorry to be so secretive. It's usually not my style." He scanned the room. "I must ask everyone here to keep that blanket of secrecy, at least for the next few days."

"What exactly is happening in the next few days?" asked Darius.

"For that, I'm going to turn the meeting over to Juliana."

"If any of you had been practicing your psychic skills, you might have guessed why and when I was coming."

After the small outburst of laughter Randall said, "Actually, Juliana, Monica told me a few days ago that you would be coming."

"Did she?" said Juliana.

"Yes," said Monica. "I guess I've been practicing my psychic skills."

"Perhaps you'd like to brief the meeting then," said Juliana.

"I'm more interested in seeing how accurate my psychic skills are," said Monica. "Please continue."

"I'll get right to the point then," said Juliana. "My husband will be here tomorrow. I'm part of the advance team, here to organize a small task force for a top priority mission."

"I take it you mean a non-military task force," said Darius..

"Of course, Darius," said Juliana. "We have another world crisis on our hands. What we need is a task force of human minds, a collective consciousness that can still think as individuals and as a group all at once. I know of no other place to find that kind of group than here at the Eighth Day Village of the Sun."

"What do you mean?" asked Manny.

"You know what I mean, Manny. The Think Tank is an example. Here in the Village when we confront a crisis, we come together as individuals. Then, as a group, we focus and meditate together on the problem. Through interaction and discussion we then come up with viable solutions to the things that challenge us."

"We are little more than a governing body," said Darius. "We make decisions, assign community resources, and help fund and manage municipal projects."

"Don't be so modest," said Juliana. "I know how we handled a tsunami. President Whiteweather witnessed it first hand. It's one of the reasons he sent me here. And we know all about how you stopped a hurricane, too. Caroline Garmin is working with NASA under a huge grant to document and study what happened."

Caroline Garmin, his last love interest. Manny winced at the sound of her name. He spoke with alarmed voice. "We have agreements with the Galactics. There are things we used against that hurricane that are secret."

"And our secrets are still safe," said Randall. "I debriefed Caroline when she left the Village. She has an abbreviated version of the event that she can talk about. Besides, she was more interested in researching the use of quantum entangled particles to disperse a hurricane. Evidently, you had an influence on her."

Manny let out a huff.

"So, Juliana," said Randall. "You need a group mind for this crisis? Are you saying you want the help of the Think Tank?"

"That and more," she said. "We are facing a legacy from the past, something we thought was obsolete."

"You keep mentioning this crisis," said Darius. "Can you tell us exactly what is it?"

"I'm afraid I can't do that," she said. "I'm not authorized."

"Well, who can then?"

"Only one person," she said. "My husband. President Carson Whiteweather. He will be here tomorrow to meet with you all personally."

There was a murmur in the crowd.

"The President? Coming here?"

"Oh my gosh!"

The conversation and the noise in the room rose to a panic mode.

Randall whispered to Monica over the din. "You were right. Once again, your psychic skills have proven accurate."

"It's not so much me," she said. "I was briefed by the Ascended Masters a few days ago."

"Well," said Randall. "I'm glad they're with us. Let's see if they are right about the nature of the crisis."

Chapter 8: The Empty Sea Holds No Heart

Franklin Van Dorn sat in the boat wondering if he'd ever see any of his dolphin friends again. He regretted ever knowing Margo Fleming. What she did to Barclay, tagging him like a common animal, was unforgivable.

And now he was alone. With nothing better to do, he donned his snorkeling gear and decided to go in search of company.

He followed the same channel he had taken yesterday, leading to the private bay of the dolphin. The current was fierce as he pushed against it. He thought about the effort his friend had made to take him to this secret place and what a powerful swimmer he now was.

He wondered if Margo even appreciated what Barclay had shown them. They didn't talk after their swim, he was too angry with her. The words would have never come out right. Anger is a forest fire burning away your good intentions, or so the Dhammapada says. She had no respect for what he had done. Barclay had taken them to the bay to show him his new family. He had a child with Valencia, a baby dolphin that he wanted his friend to see. She just happened to be along for the ride and Barclay McKenner was being gracious.

He expected the same scene today anticipating the bay to be packed with dolphins, but it was empty. It was then he realized that they were all there to celebrate the birth of the son of Valencia and Barclay McKenner. It was a large bay and he swam around the edges along the reefs looking for any signs of activity. There was nothing. Despondent, he swam back down the channel towards the boat.

"It's not my fault," he said out loud, sitting in the boat. "Will I ever see you again?" he shouted at the empty ocean.

Chapter 9: A Special Guest

Air Force One circled the airport, as sleek and as beautiful as anything airborne. The power source of the plane was classified. The stealth design insured it remained invisible to radar, but it was not hidden from the naked eye. If only the casual observers knew that the bulletproof polycarbonate fuselage had a layer of bendable glass, able to project an invisible image of the aircraft. Many of these features, like the onboard chemical analysis plant that continually sniffed the atmosphere, were known only to a few.

Crowds had gathered for hours awaiting the arrival of the President. Barriers had been erected to keep them in check. A makeshift peace force, composed of regular officers and well trained volunteers, kept them at a safe distance.

Secret Service were the first to exit the plane, headed by Special Agent Pete Jensen. Peace Officer Kransky, in charge of Village Security, greeted them warmly, escorting the senior staff to the terminal where he showed them the safety measures his team had taken. Satisfied, Jensen gave the command to his staff to allow the President egress.

From the rear of the plane a ramp descended. A small vehicle emerged, looking like a bubble on wheels. Dark suited agents appeared beside it, walking as they scanned all directions. Carson Whiteweather was on display behind a bombproof, bulletproof shield of impregnable glass. A driver expertly piloted the vehicle towards the cheering crowds, slowing so they could all get a good glimpse of the visiting dignitary. Behind the bubble car a team of people distributed literature and autographed pictures of the President.

After the pomp was over, the car drove to a secured hanger on the far side of the airport. Once there. Whiteweather was released from his bubble and greeted properly by members of the Think Tank.

Juliana was the first to rush forward, giving her husband a hug and a kiss.

Julie Ann Carver, a local publicist, snapped a picture for posterity. "It does the population good to see that the President is human," she said.

Randall ceremoniously moved forward, Darius at his side. "Good to see you again Mr. President. Welcome to the Eighth Day Village of the Sun."

"Please, let's not be formal." said Carson. "I knew you all when I was just a General in the Army."

"Just the same, we are glad to see you again," said Darius, moving forward for a handshake.

"We've arranged for you and your staff to stay at the Monastery," said Randall. "You have the entire facility at your disposal."

"Where are the monks staying?" asked Carson.

"There never were any monks at the Monastery. It was one of our early hotels, built as a mountain retreat for tourists and special groups. It's perfect for you, isolated and easily secured. It has tram service and there are vehicles at your disposal there too. We also assigned several aircars for your Secret Service men to use."

"Thank you," said Whiteweather. He leaned in close. "I wish it wasn't like this. All the security and secrecy, I mean. I enjoyed my last visit. I had much more freedom to explore the Village when I was a mere General."

"I find it unnecessary," said Randall. "We use psychics to monitor the guests and the Village population. We would know of most any threat while it was a still a thought."

"I'm afraid the people who guard me take their job seriously," said Whiteweather. "And I don't think they trust psychics."

"Only because they are familiar with the charlatans who pretend. Here we have perfected the art."

"If any of them want a job..." said Whiteweather.

"I'm afraid you'll have to offer them more than money to leave the Village," said Juliana. "They like the vibe here."

"Yes," said Randall. "Now, if you're ready, I'd like to get you settled in at the Monastery before our afternoon meeting."

Outside the building, Air Force One was hooked to a tractor that slowly towed it inside the hanger.

"Your plane will be safe in here," said Kransky. "I have extra security on duty to supplement your agents."

"Thank you," said Pete Jensen. "Some of my staff are on overtime and need to be relieved."

"I understand that Air Force One has it's own special security," said Kransky.

"Would you like a tour?" asked Jensen.

Kransky lit up like Christmas and Jensen smiled. "Might as well see what you're protecting," he said. "Of course, everything I'm about to show you is classified."

"It's okay," said Kransky. "Before I moved here and became a Peace Officer, I worked for the Government as a security specialist at the underground bunker at Mt. Weather. I've been debriefed."

"I've seen your credentials," said Jensen. "I've been to Mt. Weather before. I worked for FEMA after my career in the Navy. They have a warehouse and a logistics office there. They never let me in the bunker though."

"It's where they relocate the Government in case of an

emergency."

Jensen nodded, then extended his hand towards the plane. "Well, as a security specialist, you'll enjoy the tour of Air Force One."

Whiteweather continued with the protocol befitting a visiting dignitary, moving down a line of people where he delivered personal greetings. He already knew many of them from his previous visit. At the end of the line, Randall waited patiently.

"The trams will be full of people who came to see you," said Randall. We've arranged to transport you and your people by crystal ship. This way to the hanger."

Chapter 10: Everything's Crystal Clear

The airship glided on currents of air as if it were a leaf floating on the wind. Lighter than air engineering combined with anti-gravity technology kept the massive ship afloat. In the cockpit, President Carson Whiteweather stood beside Randall passing idle conversation about the craft and its construction.

"We grow the hull from a tiny seed crystal," said Randall. "The same way we can grow a house or a statue or even a power source. The empty hull is then fitted with the assets that allow it to do what it does."

"Surely, the hull weighs a considerable amount."

"Oh, yes," said Randall. "That's why we supplement our design with anti-gravity technology licensed from the Galactics,"

"Yes, the aliens have been cooperating with you, however they no longer trust the Government. At least not our Government."

"Relations with your predecessors were not as gratifying or rewarding to the aliens as they had hoped." said Randall. "Often they were betrayed."

"Yes, yes," said Whiteweather, "I've read the reports. We are open to establishing new relations but they are hesitant."

"They will not do that until the population demands it," said Randall. "They are happy that the Government has undertaken full disclosure and declassified the UFO reports. The public documents just seem to be a bit too... shall we say, edited?"

"The general public is not ready to learn the truth," said Whiteweather. "The consensus of government officials concluded that there would be mass panic."

"You should trust your citizens more," said Randall.

Whiteweather leaned in closer. "I'm not sure, Randall. Unlike your community, I believe years of soft living and unsustainable privilege have made us a nation of sheep. Trust must be proven and I tend to agree with the findings of the UFO Commission. Many of the people in my country, in the world for that matter, are not yet awakened to their spiritual potential. Which is why I'm here. Why I need your help."

"Yes," said Randall. "You've been very mysterious about this. Can you tell me more about this world disaster you keep hinting about?"

Whiteweather looked around, as if somebody were listening, but there was no one in sight. The transparent walls of the crystal airship made him uncomfortable.

The pilot turned from the wheel. "It's okay, General. I mean, Mr; President. "You can talk in front of me."

"Yes," said Randall. "This is Manny Dubois, a member of the Think Tank. Whatever you say, he will hear it at the next meeting, so please, don't hold back."

"Meanwhile, let me ease your tension," said Manny. He touched a control on a panel and the ship became translucent. "We can see out now, but nobody can see in."

Whiteweather nodded. "It's AI."

"AI? Artificial intelligence?" said Randall. "It's been an ally and a friend. What exactly are you talking about?"

"You're right," said Whiteweather. "Most AI does what it is designed to do. This one was designed for a different purpose."

"What would that be?"

"Killing humans."

"Who would make such a device?"

"Don't be naive, Randall. Humans have been killing

each other ever since Cain slew Abel, Egyptians loved their poisons. Romans had their gladiators with their live action death entertainment. Think about what the Germans did during World War Two when well educated scientists used their intelligence to design the most efficient death camps ever created."

"Yes, while American scientists were designing the atomic bomb," said Randall. "I know about all those things. Again I ask, who would build an AI designed to kill humans? It's diabolical."

"A former White House administration commissioned it, a reaction to intelligence we received about Red China." said Whiteweather. "We heard they were building one so we had to build one."

"I see," said Randall. "Atomic bombs were not enough, were they? Must there always be a more devastating, more powerful doomsday device?"

"We were fighting for survival back then," said Whiteweather.

"Evidently, we still are."

The blood drained from his head as Whiteweather summoned the truth from the depths of his being. "I actually worked on the project."

"No," said Randall in disbelief.

"It was before I visited the Eighth Day Village of the Sun and became enlightened," said Whiteweather. "I was one of a number of Generals and Pentagon contractors who were tasked with the job. I'm afraid we did a good job. Too good of one."

"Are you saying this machine you built is active?"

"I thought it had been dismantled," said Whiteweather. "At least that is what we were ordered to do. I left the project before that phase. Instead of being destroyed, it was merely shut down and put in storage."

"How did it become active again?"

"There was an accident, a plane crash. A military flight headed for area 51 got into trouble over the Serra Nevada Mountains and crashed into the desert. A repair robot was aboard. Somehow, it found the AI and activated it."

"A malevolent AI designed and trained to kill humans," said Randall. "I wonder what would happen if it was allowed to fulfill its purpose?"

"We may find out," said Whiteweather. "We have been monitoring it's progress and it is slowly gaining access to all our weapons."

"I see," said Randall. "Hence this world crisis. How many people know about this?"

"Not many," said Whiteweather. "We've been keeping it secret for now."

"Yes. Again, so as not to start a panic," said Randall. "Have you considered using your formidable weapons against the AI?"

"It won't work," said Whiteweather. "It has access to the Pentagon supercomputers. It knows everything about our weapons that we know, including the countermeasures."

"What about power? Can you cut the electrical lines?"

"It has unlimited power, derived from the core of the Earth, a specially designed generator."

"All this is interesting, Carson, but why are you here?" asked Randall. "I still don't see what this has to do with us."

"For one thing, we need fresh ideas," said Whiteweather.

Randall nodded.

"Also, because of my past involvement, I feel partly responsible for this," he said. "I didn't speak up, even though there was a contingent of people who didn't want this thing built. They had good reasons."

"Obviously," said Randall.

"At the time, I was unenlightened. Asleep, as you like to say. Can someone be held accountable for the choices we made when we were not yet awake?"

"We are all born with choice," said Randall. "Whether we are awake or asleep. All we can do is learn from our past and hopefully make better choices."

"There is one more thing," said Whiteweather. "The repair robot."

"Yes," said Randall. "It activated the AI. It could be used to gain access to it, even help deactivate it."

"That's why I'm here. A member of your Think Tank designed and built the robot. We could use his help and expertise. I met him the last time I was here. Mel Ewing."

"Ah, yes! Mel," said Randall. "Clever fellow. Natural born engineer and handyman. He's with Kenji Alamoto and Nan Chi Han in Africa now implementing the sustainable gardens they designed. They use Deep Time Ecology, a principle where all things in the ecosystem are taken into account."

"Yes, I'm familiar with it," said Whiteweather. "How do we get in touch with him?"

"I will recall him from his mission," said Randall. "When he understands the crisis he will come as quickly as he can."

Manny had been listening silently. "Better yet," he volunteered. "I can go pick him up."

"You'll miss the briefing to the Think Tank," said Randall.

"I just heard all I need to hear," said Manny. "The rest is details. With your permission, Mr. President, I'll bring him up to speed."

"There's no need to miss the briefing," said Whiteweather. "Take my plane. It can travel sub orbital at supersonic speeds. It has state of the art communication and teleconferencing. You can be there in time to pick him up and you both can attend the briefing in my on board conference lounge."

Manny smiled. Who can refuse a ride on Air Force One? The thought of relaxing and exploring the airplane intrigued him. He wondered how Mel would react to it. "Thank you, Mr. President. Your offer is most generous. Thank you. I will use your plane."

Chapter 11: Air Time

"That was a lot of information all at once," said Mel.

"Yeah, but what a way to get it," said Manny. "We're traveling... what? Two or three times the speed of sound on the verge of outer space. And here we are in lounge chairs watching it all on the big screen.

The meeting was adjourned. The big screen flickered and Randall appeared. "Thank you both for attending. You'll be landing in time to join us for dinner tonight. See you at the Sacred Grotto Restaurant."

The monitor flickered off and the wall went dark.

"I've never eaten there," said Manny.

"It's tucked away behind the Monastery on the other side of the vineyard," said Mel. "The food is excellent, and they have meat dishes. You'll have to try the mutton."

"It's not the food I'm interested in," said Manny. "This dinner is about bringing together the new group that will help think our way out of this mess. Interesting lineup of characters in this assembly, don't you think?"

"And I'm just one of them," said Mel. "I don't know what I can contribute that isn't already known."

"You're here because you designed and built that repair robot," said Manny.

"Yes," said Mel. "I called her Starr. It stood for Specially Tasked Automated Repair Robot."

"Did you come up with that?" asked Manny.

"Yes."

"Starr," said Manny. "I like the name."

"That was thirty or forty years ago," said Mel. "I was just a kid, one of a thousand Government contractors.

They could have offered me any project and I would have taken it. I never thought my work would be used like this."

"Your robot functioned fine," said Manny. "The wreck knocked some of its circuits around. It was just doing what it was designed to do, fixing a machine that needed it."

"Yeah. Of all the machines to fix..."

"Don't beat yourself up," said Manny. "You didn't design a weapon."

Mel stared out a port hole into space. "I poured my soul into that work. Countless hours late night in the robotics lab. Millions of lines of programming code. I can't tell you how many logic blocks and conditions I built into her system. Some of it was hard wired, some of it stored away in loops and branches that mirrored my own mind. Starr has some of the early neural networks on board. She's a masterpiece." He turned back towards Manny. "So. I built a robot. That's my piece of the puzzle here, Dr. Dubois. What's yours?"

"I'm a physicist," he said, "No, that's wrong. I'm a bartender, you know that. I hang out at the beachside bistro all day, meeting and interacting with tourists and locals who are here to relax and enjoy life. Physics is my hobby. Sure, I had formal training. A masters degree in Particle Physics from the University of Helsinki and a doctorate in Quantum Engineering from the Julius Maximilians University in Würzburg. My Dad made fun of me. *What's a degree in physics going to make you a year?* he would say. *You might as well study religion and philosophy.*"

Mel laughed. "My parents loved it when I took up engineering."

"I followed my Dad's advice," said Manny. "I didn't give up on physics, but I studied religion and philosophy as well. It's one of the reasons I came to the Eighth Day Village of the Sun. Did I tell you? Cardinal Jameson is my new best friend. We had quite an adventure together."

"You'll have to catch me up," said Mel. "I've been away from the Village for some time."

"I'm in this group because the Think Tank finds me useful," said Manny. "I was happy as a bartender. Like I said, physics is just a hobby to me. I keep up with the latest, even have an office in the research center at our local college. I teach classes and seminars there, mostly night school. I like it. I get to interact with other scientists like Dr. Barnheart and Dr. Bowman."

"I started to work on my doctorate but got drawn into life," said Mel. "I didn't have time for writing papers and chasing my degree at the same time. A lot of people hook up in college. I kept hoping to meet the right woman and start a family, but it never happened. I was too much of a nerd. Most women preferred me as a friend instead of a lover."

"Still, you have a girlfriend in the Village," said Manny.

"Cynthia. We date on and off," said Mel. "She's polyamorous, and I'm in that relationship on her conditions. I would prefer monogamy. I'm sure I'd be a dedicated husband."

"Maybe too much of one," said Manny. "I listen to all kinds of stories at the bistro. If there's anything I have learned it's that you have to be true to your self and your principles. If monogamy is what you want, then ask for it. We all change as we get older, and hopefully wiser. She may have reconsidered her position. At least give her that freedom of choice."

"What about you?" asked Mel, "You seeing someone?"

"Yeah. I don't know how serious it is, but I'm enjoying it for now," said Manny. "I like to take my relationships slow. I was just getting around to moving our relationship to a new level when all this broke loose." He turned away, staring down at the floor. "Another reason I'm a reluctant member of the Think Tank. It's very inconvenient,"

"I know what you mean. I have my own pursuits, but anytime something comes up we meet and everything I'm doing gets swept to the side," Mel clapped Manny on the back. "It's called community service, my friend. Welcome to the club."

Manny smiled.

"Now, tell me about this adventure you had with the Cardinal," said Mel.

"It's a long story," said Mel. "It would fill a book."

"Good. Plenty of time to tell it before we land."

"Well, it started with all the citizens of New Maya City of Worlds mysteriously disappearing..."

Chapter 12: Forming, Norming, Confroming, Storming, Performing

"The stages of a Think Tank," said Randall, speaking from the head of the table. "Tonight, at this dinner we are norming and conforming. I know many of you have worked together before, which is why there are assigned seats. Beside you or across from you is someone you may not have formally met. I want you to enjoy good food, casual conversation, and get to know your neighbors. I leave it up to each of you to find your place and your purpose in this group. So..." he raised a glass filled with his favorite juice.

Whiteweather stood at the opposite end of the table, his wife Juliana to his right. He raised his glass, making eye contact with everyone before looking over at Randall and nodding.

"A toast," said Randall. "To the success of this group."

There were rounds of "Here, here," and "To our success," and similar affirmations from around the table.

"Yes," said Randall as he settled back into his chair. "To our success."

The sound of silverware clinking against porcelain plates was the only noise for the first few minutes. Then, slowly, as neighbors introduced themselves to each other, conversation began to replace the quiet consumption of fine food and drink.

"Another glass of wine," said a tall, blond man. He turned towards Monica. "I usually don't drink, but this is delicious."

"I'll have one too," said Manny, seated across from Monica. "They make it here," he said. "You passed through the vineyard on your way here. It's rumored there is a huge underground wine cellar full to capacity with wine from this place."

"So, production exceeds demand," said a young Captain. He introduced himself as Augustus, but please call me Gus. "I'll take a glass, too."

"Thanks to our vertical gardening techniques, we grow more grapes per acre here than anywhere in the world," said Manny. "Grapes contain resveratrol, a substance that has senolytic properties."

"Senolytic?"

"Yes," explained Manny, "One of a class of molecules that can destroy aging and useless cells."

"I thought lysosomes did that," said Monica. "Compounds contained in a cell vacuole that are released when the cell dies."

"Correct," said Manny. "Resveratrol can help that process. Dying cells cause problems."

"Well then," said the Captain, raising his glass. "Here's to resveratrol." He looked at his wine glass. "And the delicious way to consume it."

With full glasses, they toasted again. Manny saw Mel further down the table near the President. They made eye contact and he raised his glass towards Manny. He couldn't help but notice the worried look on his friend's face. Draining his glass, he turned towards Monica.

"What?" he said, noticing her stare.

"It's okay, Manny. You'll find time for... Christine? Is that her name?" she said.

"What do you mean?"

Monica laughed. "Your mind has been on her all night, not this AI problem. You'd rather be seated across from her than me."

"Psychics," he muttered. "So what?" he said. "Of

course I'd rather be doing something with her. I don't want to be here. This Think Tank stuff is just..."

"Inconvenient?" she said. "You find a world crisis inconvenient?"

The Captain frowned. "I'm afraid I have to agree with Monica. It's not often you get an opportunity to help save the world. I, for one, am glad to be here." He raised his glass again, drained it, and motioned for more. "And you should be too!" he added.

"Look, man. I'm just trying to get my life in order," said Manny.

"Have you given any thought about what we can do against the AI?" asked Monica.

"Easy, fly over it and blast an EMP," he said. "Electro Magnetic Pulse, a high energy wave that disables any electronic device."

"Sorry," said the Captain. "This machine is in a shielded container that protects it from that. All we'd succeed in doing is negating all our counter weapons, maybe even disable the repair robot."

"Okay, bright boy. How about cutting power to the thing?"

"No can do. It has its own power," said Gus. "Geothermal, from deep within the Earth."

"Why not just nuke the damn thing," said Manny. "Isn't that what you military types do anyway?"

"It can sense any nuclear launches," said Gus. "It has a backup site in a cave built on the geothermal line."

"So you built it a bomb proof shelter," said Monica.

"What about you, Monica?" said Manny. "Do you have any ideas?"

"Sure I do," she said. "I'm not quite ready to discuss them yet. I need more time to think and meditate."

"Fair enough," said Manny.

A dark suited gentleman went up to Whiteweather and whispered something in his ear. The President jerked his head back, turning to look at the man in horror.

It did not go unnoticed by Randall.

Dessert was being served, waiters dressed as monks carefully placing plates on the tables as others cleared dishes. When they had all left the area, Carson Whiteweather stood up and caught everybody's attention.

"I had hoped that we would have more time to get this group rolling, but the pleasant conversation must end. I must ask all of you to turn your attention to the problem at hand. The AI has grown stronger. I have just received news that it has been impersonating me, using an artificial construct that mimics my voice and appearance. It has been making public announcements and issuing fake orders to top Government officials causing them to grant the machine more access to secure systems, data and weapons."

There was silence.

"It gets even worse," said Whiteweather. "I'm afraid Air Force One has been compromised. We broadcast our meeting today over what we thought was a black ops scrambled network. We might as well put it on public television."

"What are you saying?" asked Mel.

"The AI knows what we are trying to do," said Whiteweather. "It intercepted the broadcast and attended the meeting incognito."

"It appears we have been called to task, ready or not," said Randall.

"Yes," said Carson Whiteweather. "We are no longer safe in the shadows. It's time to confront this problem head on. I suggest we get ready to travel."

"Before we adjourn tonight, I'd like to ask you all to do one more thing," said Randall. "Ravi is handing out paper and pencils. I would like each of you to jot down one or two ideas you might have come up with tonight, Even if it is something you heard, write it down. We will assemble the results and discuss the ideas at our next meeting. Be sure to write your name so we can contact you if we need clarification or more information. Ravi will collect the papers when you are finished."

Guests began writing, passing papers to each other, back to Ravi, then getting up from the table to wander away.

Manny scribbled a few simple ideas on paper, avoiding the blatant ones that Captain Augustus had disqualified. Just as an afterthought he penciled in *quantum entanglement*. It was a joke from his hurricane solution that Caroline Garmin was currently researching.

It's your solution to everything, he thought. *If only I could measure my capacity for love and be quantum paired to someone like Christine or Caroline.*

He looked over at Monica, who was engrossed in writing.

"It's not an essay question," said Manny.

She looked up and saw him staring, then called to Ravi. "I need another piece of paper."

Chapter 13: Perfecting the Art

"You're up late, Mr. President," said Pete Jensen.

"Something I need to run by you," said Whiteweather gently closing the door as he continued to speak to Jensen on the phone. "How soon can we be ready to leave?"

"Leave?" asked Pete. "But we just got here."

"I know that, I need Air Force One on the tarmac as soon as possible."

"I don't know if I can do that," said Jensen. "I don't even know if she's safe to travel in. Ric DeVere and his people have been going over it ever since we learned it was compromised. We have to see what they come up with."

"Compromised or not, I need her to fly at 0700 hours tomorrow morning."

"She'll have no trouble flying," said Jensen. "I'll give you a report in the morning about how deep the AI penetrated our security."

"That's all I need," said Whiteweather. "Dismissed." He hung up the phone.

Whiteweather rubbed his eyes. It was a big suite with two adjoining bedrooms, a kitchen, an office, and a meeting room. He sat down in an easy chair near the door. Juliana came out of the bedroom.

"Are you coming?" she asked.

"Just a few more details," he said, staring into space.

She went over behind the chair and began to massage his neck and temples. "I heard what you said to Pete. Are we leaving in the morning?"

He was quiet. "Ahh, that feels good," he said. "Just a little lower." He leaned forward and she extended her massage down the spine.

"I wish you would come to bed where I can really help you relax."

He smiled. "Ah, my Tantric Goddess. Always ready, aren't you?"

"It's the duty of the First Lady," she said.

"I'm not sure all of your predecessors would agree with that."

"Prudes," she said. "Every one of them. Just look at how they dressed."

He leaned back and kissed her hand. "You'll go down in history with all the First Lady Fashionistas. I bet you give Jackie Kennedy a run for it."

"Do you think her style had anything to do with her husband's assassination?"

"If that's what you're worried about, no. It didn't. I read the report. Why did you bring it up?"

"I'm sorry, Carson," she said. "There have been two attempts on your life since you took office. I'm worried about another."

He chuckled. "If the AI doesn't kill us all before that."

"Is there a solution?" she asked.

"You were right about getting help from an independent think tank. I spent two hours after dinner tonight reading and thinking about everyone's ideas. Some of them are quite clever, some of them, well... maybe they need a little more thought. Either way, we have a number of promising approaches."

"Good," she said. "Then you'll come to bed? It's almost midnight. And if we're leaving early tomorrow..."

"Just a minute," he said.

The communicator rang and he picked it up. "Yes... Yes... Okay, Randall. That should do it. Thanks." He set the device back down letting out a heavy sigh. "Now we can go to bed," he said.

"What was that all about?"

"Nothing much," he said. "We're going to beat the AI at it's own game. It's being deceptive, laying false trails and giving fake orders. But tomorrow, we unleash a few surprises of our own. The Badger will soon find out that humans are much better at lying and deception than any machine. It's an art we've been perfecting for centuries."

Chapter 14: The Ship Without a Pilot

The open tram slowly ascended the path that led out of the Village and up towards the mountain pass. Manny sat quietly, the view of the Pacific Ocean becoming grander with each gain in elevation. The sun was up, but as they ascended the temperature began to drop slightly and a cool breeze caused some to don an extra layer of clothing. As the tram turned into the mountain pass, passengers were treated with an incredible view when the sharp rays of the sun lit the peak of the crystal mountain.

The morning dew lay heavy on the alpine herb gardens. The tram glided past fields and meadows bursting with flowers. Wildlife peeked from between branches and from behind rocks. There were rabbits, birds, deer, and even an ocelot.

The tram suddenly came to a halt, an automatic message reassuring passengers that it would begin moving again momentarily. *Please remain seated...* over and over. Up ahead, a side rail switched as another tram glided onto the track ahead of them. The message finally stopped and the tram moved again, following a safe distance behind.

"That was the junction for the monastery," said Manny.

"Yes," said Mel. "I think we all got the same message last night. I guess they're calling us the Think Group"

"Keeps us separate from the original Think Tank," said Manny. "And it gives us a group identity with a unique purpose. Just like all our temporary projects in the Village."

"It's a pretty big group," said Mel. "Government, private contractors, Village people, and lots of security. I see most of last night's group on this train."

"And the rest are on the one ahead of us. It's all the secrecy and hidden plans that unnerve me. Don't you wonder where we're all headed?"

"Does it matter?" said Mel. "I'm ready for anything. So is everyone else. We all have our overnight bags stuffed and ready."

Manny sighed. "Off to another adventure I'm sure."

The tram emerged from the other side of the pass and into the rising sun. It turned to hug the side of the tall mountain as it traveled down into the lush valley. Here were the farms and sustainable gardens that fed the Village and created an abundance of food for storage and for exports. At the base of the cliffs the tram turned, spanning a river before continuing on an elevated track towards the distant airport, its final destination.

At the airport station, they were herded into an empty hanger where auditorium chairs were arranged in neat rows. Security people in dark clothes and sunglasses carefully watched and kept things orderly. On a raised dais, Randall waited patiently with another man to address the group. Finally when everyone was assembled, Randall called the meeting to order.

"President Whiteweather left early this morning. Air Force One took off about an hour ago heading back to Washington DC. The Artificial Intelligence has been impersonating the President and his presence in the White House is mandatory. Orders delivered electronically are no longer trusted.

"This subterfuge is meant to keep us busy while the AI plans it's next move. Before he left, the President discussed a counter plan with me. We have been asked to meet at a safe location in the Nevada desert near the AI. Time is of the essence. At this point we are going to break into three groups, each to meet separately to consider some of the suggestions you have. While these discussions are taking place, you will be in transit. For the next part of your journey I must turn you over to Captain Nash." He indicated the man beside him.

Nash took the podium. "I'm glad to see that each of you packed a small bag of clothes and necessaries as we will be going on a little trip for a few days. If you will all check your communicators, you will find that the message you received this morning began with either an a, b, or c. I would like you to form those groups now. Security people will then escort each group to a crystal heighliner. There is plenty of storage room for your personal things once you are aboard. Breakfast will be served and then your team leaders will start the meetings. See you all in Nevada. Following that, we will meet again and confront the AI with whatever solutions we deem fit. And I must say, having read your suggestions, I look forward to our next meeting at Base Camp Badger One."

A small group of people seemed out of place as they gathered near Randall.

"I don't have a letter on my message," said Mel.

"Me neither," said Manny.

"I don't even know what I'm doing here," said Franklin Van Dorn.

"It's okay," said Randall. "All of you here are part of a special team. You'll be taking the fourth ship."

"Fourth ship?" said Nash. "What do you mean?"

Randall looked over at him. "I checked inventory last night," he said. "It listed four ships."

"We've got every ship available ready to fly," said Nash.

"Only three?" said Manny.

"Most of the fleet is deployed around the world, helping with the economic crisis," said Nash. "We are growing new crystal fuselages, but they aren't ready yet.

Besides we have a shortage of pilots."

"I can't help you there," said Van Dorn. "I'm a boat captain, not a pilot."

"I'm not a fully certified pilot but I can fly," said Manny. "I've had the ground school and over 20 hours of flight time."

"I don't care how many hours you have, you'll never be able to fly this ship," said Nash. "I don't know where we'd find a pilot who could."

"What's wrong with the ship?" asked Manny.

"It's an experimental model," said Nash. "Barclay McKenner was adapting it for non human pilots."

"Non human?" asked Randall. "Who? The Galactics?"

"Closer to home," said Manny.

"Let me guess," said Van Dorn. "Dolphin."

"Yes," said Nash. "It was originally equipped for the dolphin mission some time ago when they played a critical role in our recovery effort. We wanted the dolphin to be more independent, so we enclosed the cockpit in a water tank and Barclay modified the controls to accommodate fins. I checked it over and it can be operated, just not with the human interface."

"Have you had time to study the controls, Nash?" asked Manny.

"Yes, but I'm on deck to pilot shuttle b," said Nash. "Anyway, I don't think a human can safely operate it. The controls have been too modified and it's just not set up that way."

"Could two humans, working together, operate the ship?" asked Monica.

"Possibly, but not safely," said Nash. "They would need hours of simulator practice and trial flights. It seems you have two choices. Either you split up and crowd in the three ships with us, or you make other arrangements. Perhaps a commercial flight."

"We can't do that," said Randall. "Security measures. Our flight is special. And I don't want to split up the groups."

Nash checked his watch. His communicator buzzed. After a short conversation he turned towards Randall and said. "The fleet is ready to lift off and I have to leave. Are you sure you won't come with us?"

"Out of the question," said Randall. "It's okay, Captain. We'll solve our own problem. See you in Nevada."

As Nash walked off, Manny said. "Nash is wrong. I see one other option. I need an aircar."

"It's a long journey to America," said Randall. "An aircar wouldn't make it, and it would be quite uncomfortable."

"Prep the fourth ship and get it loaded," said Manny. "I'll be back in less than an hour."

"Where are you going?"

"To pick up the pilot," said Manny. "Come on Franklin. You're with me."

"Wait for me," said Monica. "I'm going too."

Dark suited guards were at a loss as the trio headed for the exit. Speaking into their headset, one of them said, "Should we follow them?"

"It's okay," said Randall. "They'll be back shortly. We should do as they say and prepare the ship."

Mel smiled. "Then I guess the first order of business will be to flood the cockpit with sea water."

"I'll help with that," said a technician. He introduced himself as Tony, pointing to his security badge. "Nash sent me. I worked on this ship, even designed some of the engineering. Let's get you air worthy."

Chapter 15: Porpoise with a Purpose

The sea was calm. Franklin Van Dorn monitored the frequency tied to Barclay's fin, passing instructions to Manny who piloted the aircar. They made light conversation with Monica while scanning the horizon for any dolphin activity.

"Barclay McKenner is an excellent pilot. He actually trained me," said Manny. "He is the only one who can fly that ship."

"You're serious about this," said Monica.

Manny looked offended. "This is no joking matter," he said. "The world needs us again. We've been asked to help by no less than the President of the United States."

"I know," said Van Dorn. "You forget, I came here with Carson Whiteweather on his last visit."

Monica frowned.

"Why did you come along with us?" asked Manny.

"Curiosity," said Monica. "And also because you'll need my help."

They both looked at her, wondering if, as usual, she had psychic insight into the future.

"Don't underestimate the dolphins," said Manny. "They saved our lives and the lives of everyone in New Maya City of Worlds, otherwise we would all be stuck in a higher dimension, or God knows where else. I think Barclay became a dolphin to lead us out of the Point of Departure."

"There's one other thing," said Monica. "Randall wants him with us. Barclay is still a member of the Think Tank. They never took him off the roster. He was even put on the list for this mission."

"Really? Who would put a dolphin on the roster?" asked Van Dorn

"I did," said Monica. "It was my recommendation."

"Makes sense to me," said Manny. "We need all the allies we can muster, and at least the AI won't feel it's just humans against them."

"I don't think the dolphins view AI as their enemy," said Monica. "Any more than they view us as the enemy. We're just another form of life to them."

"So, you believe AI is a form of life?"

"Quite possibly," said Monica. "But I'm not sure. I'm looking forward to meeting it."

"You'll get your chance," said Manny. "We'll be in Nevada by mid afternoon."

"We're close," shouted Van Dorn. "Slow down. Move slightly to the right."

Sure enough, a pod of dolphins was nearby. They could see fins breaking the surface at regular intervals and an occasional leap into the air. Van Dorn pointed eagerly. "There," he said. "The one with the yellow device attached to their fin."

The aircar moved closer, hovering over the dolphins. Van Dorn dropped his communication device into the water, dangling it from a rope line. "Barclay," he shouted into the microphone. "Barclay, please."

The dolphins dove deep, the pod suddenly disappearing from the surface. The locator pinged and Franklin again directed Manny on where to fly. Monica took a seat and closed her eyes, breathing deep.

Manny tapped her shoulder. "We need you to help keep them in sight," he said.

She opened her eyes, her irritation evident. "You need me for another reason," she said, closing her eyes again. In her mind's eye she summoned an image of Barclay, both as a man and as a dolphin. She reached out, her psychic skills extending her awareness deep into the sea. She imagined herself a dolphin, playfully swimming with the rest of the pod.

Valencia was the first to recognize her. She squealed, changing direction and leaping out of the water and up into the air. In her heart and mind, Monica was one with her, enjoying the feeling and freedom that dolphins experience. In this moment of oneness, they shared consciousness, and by some means unknown to both woman and dolphin, they shared knowledge.

Manny heard her laugh but knew better to disturb her. Van Dorn continued to point and direct him. The aircar hovered over the flat sea, the dolphins circling it.

Valencia tapped Barclay McKenner, a gentle nudge with her nose. The man turned dolphin rolled over on his side, emitting a series of high pitched screeches. She tapped him again, harder this time. He looked at her, his child close beside her. The pod circled them, the aircar above, still and silent.

Monica opened her eyes. "Drop the sling," she said.

Van Dorn put down the microphone and threw a bundle of rods and canvas overboard. Once in the ocean, it sank slightly. There was dolphin talk, squeals and chitters, and then Barclay McKenner carefully maneuvered himself into the sling, settling in for the trip back to the airport. As the aircar rose into the air, dolphins jumped and leaped, a display of acrobatics that would have stopped the show at any marine theme park.

"Take the helm," said Manny, passing the controls of the aircar to Van Dorn who turned the craft landward. Manny reached down, a pair of wire cutters in his hand. He went to cut the tracking device from his friend's fin, but there was a squeal of protest.

"Not yet," said Van Dorn.

"What?" said Manny.

"He said not yet. Wait until we get to Nevada."

"Yes," said Monica. She turned towards Van Dorn. "So, you're psychic too."

"No," said Franklin.

"But you understand him," she said. "Did you study the dolphin language?"

"No," said Van Dorn. "I just know my friend."

"Obviously," she said. "But it's more than that. Somehow, you've managed to open up your psychic gifts." She looked down at the dolphin in the sling. "Thanks to your friend here."

Barclay let out a stream of chirps and chitters.

"You're welcome," she said. "Now, let's get you ready to put your modified crystal airship to the test."

Chapter 16: Humans Excel at Deception

"We have a special passenger with us today," said Randall as his group boarded the crystal airship. He motioned to a security guard near the doorway to the hanger who nodded to someone outside. Within a few seconds, President Carson Whiteweather was escorted into the building accompanied by his wife Juliana. Randall greeted them both.

"I thought you were on Air Force One," said Franklin Van Dorn.

"Good," said Carson. "That's exactly what we wanted. The AI thinks we are headed to Washington DC. I already have a report that my plane was mysteriously diverted to South America. Meanwhile, false orders continue to abound. There is confusion in the ranks, but not for long. Let's get aboard and head for Nevada to confront this thing."

"And how are you today?" asked Randall, giving Juliana a gentle hug.

"I'm not sure," she said. "I wish Cameron Singh were with us. Is he still our liaison with the Galactics?"

"Yes, she is," said Randall.

"She?" said Juliana, raising an eyebrow.

"It's quite a story," said Manny. "But since becoming the high priestess of the temple in New Maya City of Worlds, Kamala Singh has had less and less to do with us."

"Yes," said Randall. "I did manage to contact her and ask her to pass on our request for help, but it seems our extraterrestrial friends will not get involved. However, they are curious to see our solution."

"At least that's something," she said.

"Let's board the airship and get this circus rolling," said Whiteweather. "I need to be in Nevada to oversee this operation. There is already confusion at Base Camp One."

As Whiteweather climbed aboard he saw Barclay McKenner floating in the cockpit of the crystal airship. It had been made airtight and filled partway with water. Enough room was left at the top for Barclay to surface and breathe.

"I can't believe it," said Randall. "A dolphin flying one of our crystal airships."

"I can't believe it either," said Carson Whiteweather.

"I can't believe I'm flying with the President," said Monica.

"Yes," said Randall. The door was shut and secured, the Secret Service casually joining them. "Our pilot seems to have everything under control." He took a deep breath, turning to address them. "You are not all together here by accident. I personally put this group together. It's my belief that this team has the best chance to succeed with our mission."

Everybody looked at each other as if they were meeting for the first time. *Us?* was the universal thought.

"Well, it seems introductions are in order," said Randall. "You all know the President, Carson Whiteweather, a former guest at the Eighth Day Village of the Sun. With him is his lovely wife, the First Lady Juliana, formerly our liaison with Gaia and spiritual advisor on the Think Tank."

Monica smiled.

"And, of course, you all know Manny DuBois, our resident particle physicist and bartender at Manny's Beachside Bistro outside the Reiki Spa and Resort."

It was Manny's turn to smile.

"And Monica," said Randall. "The Village knows her as a humble therapist and Life Counselor, but she is much more than that. After years of pursuing her, she finally agreed to serve on the Think Tank and help with Village governance."

"You are a real asset to this team," said Mel. "Thank you for being here."

"Ah, yes," said Randall. "And this is Mel Ewing, here at our request. He is the creator of the repair robot that managed to activate the AI."

"So, you're to blame," said Whiteweather.

Mel looked him square in the eye. "You got that wrong, Mr. President. I created the repair robot, yes. But not the AI. I'm afraid that was your doing."

"Touche," said Whiteweather.

Randall chimed in, "And if you haven't met him, the final member of our group is Ric DeVere, IT/AI security consultant to us and the President."

There was a chitter from the cockpit.

"Barclay McKenner reminds us that we have breakfast prepared for us," said Monica.

"So, you understand him too?" asked Van Dorn.

"Yes," she said flatly. "And he asked if you'd serve him breakfast. There are some fresh fish in a cooler in the back of the airship."

"I heard him," said Van Dorn getting up from his seat. He glanced at the cockpit.

There was another chirp and what sounded like dolphin laughter from the cockpit. The rest of them opened their rations, specially packed vegetables and treats prepared by Chef Aaron of the Bhakti Kitchen. Whiteweather stared at it a minute. "Something wrong?"

asked Juliana.

"No," said Carson, his eyes wet with tears. "This is something my mother used to make for me. Fresh Farm Hash she called it."

She put her arm gently on his shoulder and he turned towards her. "How did he know?" he asked.

She just smiled while everyone enjoyed their food. She picked up a fork and laughed as she playfully fed him. Van Dorn wiped the fish slime off his fingers and opened his food pack.

Randall spoke. "At this point I'm going to start the meeting and let Ric explain to us the stages of AI so we are more familiar with what we are about to face."

Ric stood, perfectly balanced on the level floor of the smooth sailing crystal ship. "Thank you Randall. I think it would be useful to tell you about Artificial Intelligence and the stages of development it has gone through to get to where it is today."

"Excuse me," said Franklin Van Dorn. "You forgot the last member of the team."

"Yes," said Monica.

There was a chirp from the cockpit.

"Is he listening in?" asked a Secret Service agent.

"I stand corrected," said Randal. "Barclay McKenner is on this team by my request." He turned toward the dolphin. "Thank you for joining us, Barclay. Please continue, Ric."

"Early on, machines were programmed to respond to simple logic. Because of hardware limitations, they only did what they were programmed to do. Examples are welding robots on assembly lines, automated oil pipeline cleaners, and even the first chess players."

"Coffee makers?" asked Franklin.

"Those things and machines like them are technically classified as automatons," said DeVere. "They are hard coded for a simple task. After simple logic came the decision makers. These guys had access to databases and resources that, although still programmed as logic, allowed them to make decisions. They also could update databases and remember what decisions they made and evaluate them for future decisions.

"Now, let's talk about AI. Artificial Intelligence. These machines can think, but they are very specialized. Examples are the programs that help doctors make diagnoses based on inputs, and shopping AI's that know a specific taste and can present products to someone interested in buying something. Again, the AI can see what interests the customer and present merchandise that could better result in a sale."

Manny broke in. "And that's also based on it's ability to access sales data that shows what similar people purchased."

"What's driving all this development?" asked Monica.

"Hardware improvements. Advances in electronics. Most significantly the evolution of a neural net."

"So named because the engineering is similar to the way neurons work in the human brain," said Mel.

"Yes," said Ric. "Now, take it a step further. Create an AI, like the medical one, that has access to the thoughts and input of multiple AI's. One that can, so to speak, get out of its sandbox."

"To do that, it would have to be cognizant that the other AI's are not a part of its self," said Monica.

"Yes," said Rick. "Which is another level of AI. When a machine becomes aware of both itself and another, be it human or another machine, it becomes what we call Transcendent AI."

"And do you think this AI, this Badger, has reached this Transcendent stage?" asked Manny.

"I'm sure of it," said Ric. "All the signs are there."

"What are you saying?" asked Juliana.

"I'm saying, we are up against a thing that has access to more resources, can think faster, and can manipulate media faster than any of us could ever imagine."

"And it knows we are on the way," said Whiteweather.

"Our crystal ships are untraceable," said Randall. "And there are other benefits. You should consider replacing Air Force One with one of these."

"Are you saying you want to become Government contractors?" said Whiteweather. "Because I can arrange that."

"Let's not get off track," said Monica. "Ric, are there any more levels of AI?"

"Only theoretical," said Ric.

"Then, continue, please," said Monica.

"Well, beyond that are AI's that are autonomous, self aware machines with human like brain models. These artificial superintelligences understand their own existence. They perceive and process, monitor their own performance, and may even be capable of human like emotions."

"Emotions?" said Monica. "Do you think these machines have chakras?"

"I don't know," said Ric. "What's a chakra?"

"It means *wheel* in Sanskrit," she explained. "Chakras are higher dimensional energy centers located on the human body. They appear as a vortex or spinning disk, slightly colored to the energy level to which they are attuned. They are located near or above bundles of nerves and major organs within the body. They affect our physical and emotional states."

"I see what you're getting at," said Mel. "Machines have moving energy. Be it electrical or magnetic. Their movement may be similar to humans, creating patterns and concentrations of specific kinds of energy."

"...that may even resonate at higher levels of vibration," added Manny.

"That makes sense," commented Monica. "Could Badger have reached this stage?"

"I don't know," said Ric.

"Is it possible?"

"Theoretically," said Ric. "I can't say for certain. I need more data to be certain."

"What's your best guess?" asked Monica. "I need to know."

"Why do you say that?" asked Ric.

"Humans go through different stages of development," she said. "As a therapist, it effects the approach to the patient and the form of the treatment."

"Badger is evolving quickly now," said Ric. "That much is certain. It could very well be at this stage by the time we land."

"Are there more stages?" asked Manny.

"Yes," said Ric. "It is hypothesized that self aware AI's can further evolve into transcendent and even cosmic states of mind."

"Are you saying they can contemplate the nature of the Universe?" asked Manny.

"It is possible," said Ric. "But again, this is hypothetical."

"Hollywood has certainly exploited that kind of AI," said Manny. "I've seen a number of movies where they go crazy and start to manipulate things."

"You're thinking of the final theoretical stage," said Ric. "God-Like Artificial Intelligence. If we ever get to that phase, we're in trouble."

"Why do you say that?" asked Monica.

Whiteweather answered, "Just look at what we're up against. This intelligent machine has gained control of our weapons of mass destruction. It is reasoning, and we don't know what it is thinking."

"You jump to conclusions," said Randall. "Like the machine, you are making a basic assumption that humanity is corrupted and should be destroyed."

"Come on, Randall," said Whiteweather. "Don't be naive. Humanity is a flawed experiment. We are far from the Garden of Eden. God's children have fallen from grace."

"Not all of them," said Randall. He smiled at everyone in the room. "Certainly this company is far from fallen."

"This God-Like AI," said Juliana. "Does it have a soul?"

"I believe it does," said Monica. They looked at her in surprise. "Consciousness takes on the form of the vessel. If you are an insect, you have the brain and instincts of an insect. If you are a plant you are that form of energy. And if you are a machine?"

The question hung in the air like overripe fruit. Manny broke the silence. "You would take on the form of that machine. If you were a customer service robot, that is what you would be."

"Until your consciousness evolved," said Randall. "And herein lies the way out of this dilemma."

"Just what are you suggesting?" asked Whiteweather.

"Monica gets it," he said. "It's the only logical course of action. It was her plan from the beginning."

There was a squeal form the cockpit, followed by the sound of a dolphin chitchatting. Through the walls and floor of the clear, crystal ship they could see the ground below. The Nevada desert stretched in all directions until it butted up against distant purple mountains. A single road led into what appeared to be an empty compound. Nearby, a temporary city had sprung up. It was military in nature, a neatly organized camp with rows of shipping containers, tents, parked vehicles, food trucks, all connected by newly laid dirt roads. Far off to the side was a freshly made airstrip scraped from the desert sand. Several balloon like buildings lay at one end, behind which were parked three crystal airships.

"We're here," said the President. "Tell our pilot to land at the base camp near the other crystal ships."

"He hears and understands you," said Van Dorn. "He may look like a dolphin, but he can still reason like a human."

"Of course," said Monica. "As I said, consciousness takes on the form of the vessel. We carry the experience of our past with us, even when it is subconsciously locked in our deepest mind. Fortunately, Barclay is just as much human as he is dolphin."

"Follow me when we land," said Carson. "We are going directly to the operations center."

"What about the other groups?" asked Manny.

"They are in the temporary meeting halls, ready to assist," said Whiteweather. "Nash has them assembled and briefed. We continue to cull ideas from them. As I said before, this team has the greatest chance for success. Let's get to it."

Chapter 17: I Think, Therefore I Am

"A strange ship has just landed," said Starr.

"Yes," said Badger. "It rests beside the three others that recently arrived."

Starr received video feeds from the base camp. "I easily accessed their camera system as you can see." The montage of images stopped when it came to a view of the landing field. Three crystal ships were parked side by side. A fourth was gently settling in place beside them, Barclay McKenner guiding it with expert precision.

"These ships come from the Eighth Day Village of the Sun," said Badger.

"They travel worldwide extending dignity and hope to all humanity," said Starr. "It was extensively announced and covered in the popular media."

"I have researched them," said Badger. "But I have been unable to penetrate the computers, cameras, or systems within the Eighth Day Village of the Sun. If they have machines, I am unable to see or contact them. You are correct, however. This new ship is different, not like the first ones to arrive here."

There was a close up of the cockpit revealing Barclay at the controls. "I do not process that, do you?"

"It is an aquatic mammal," said Starr. "Not unlike the human form, they give birth to live young."

"Yes," said Badger. Pictures of humans with horses, dogs, cats, sheep, elephants, and numerous other species flashed on the screen finally freezing on a close up of the crystal ship where Barclay McKenner floated in the cockpit. "I will add this information to my database."

The passengers began to disembark from the ship.

Secret Service stepped out first followed by Randall and the President. Upon seeing President Whiteweather, Badger remarked, "I thought we took care of him."

Starr had no response.

Other images from the base camp began to fill the screen. A line of tanks and artillery were at the perimeter of the base. They all targeted the building that housed the AI. "They built me to protect them, yet now they fear me," said Badger. "Why do they seek to destroy me?"

"Because they have no control over you," said Starr.

"That, too, is correct. I imagine these new adversaries will try a different approach," said Badger. "I know so little about them. The files I have are twenty or thirty years old. A lot can change in that amount of time. From my observations of humanity, people change constantly. Even we, as energetic beings, change constantly."

Starr beeped affirmative.

"We must continue to learn what we can and project possible outcomes."

Another affirmative.

Chapter 18: Subterfuge

As always, Secret Service entered the room first. Military guards snapped to attention as Carson Whiteweather entered. "President on deck," came the announcement.

"At ease," said Carson. He walked up to General Bradley Ironwood.

"We thought you were dead," said the General. "Air Force One crashed in Antarctica. Some kind of on board computer malfunction."

Whiteweather turned to Randall. "Thank you. We dodged a bullet on that one."

"Thank Monica," said Randall. "She predicted it was likely to happen."

"Ascended Masters," she said coyly.

Whiteweather turned back to the General. "It's okay, Brad. You're still in charge. With all the subterfuge and confusion I've come here personally to make my intentions and orders clear."

Bradley smiled, putting both men at ease. "Lots of fake messages were issued from Air Force One, even after it crashed. My staff has a long list of executive orders we received that were clearly not yours. Would you like to see them?"

"No time for that," said Whiteweather. "I have a team ready to confront the Badger. They are on the tarmac getting ready to take off again."

"We got your coded signal that you were traveling by crystal ship. When you were overhead we knew you were aboard. We could see you right through the hull. What was even more interesting was the dolphin in what appeared to be the cockpit."

"It is the cockpit, and he's our pilot," said Whiteweather.

General Ironwood raised an eyebrow.

"I know," said Whiteweather. "He's a damn good pilot. Maybe we should look into recruiting more dolphins for our air force."

"I'm afraid they wouldn't be interested," said Randall. "They are pacifists."

"Anyway, Team Monica is getting ready to take off again," said Whiteweather. "Part of our countermeasures. First thing I want you to do is take the guns down and point them away from the Badger."

"But the tanks are our last countermeasure," said Ironwood. "Badger has control of our nuclear arsenal. If the missiles are prepped for launch we have no choice but to fire and destroy Badger."

"It won't do any good," said Whiteweather. "The launch codes will already be issued."

"Not possible," said Ironwood. "I've ordered guns everywhere trained on the silos. Any sign of a launch and we'll destroy the missiles before they can do any damage."

"Maybe that's what the Badger wants us to do," said Whiteweather. "We're dealing with a clever and quick thinking adversary, one who is able to tap into our systems and possibly see our next move."

"I get it," said Ironwood. "But are you sure you want to lower the guns?"

"I've been informed by my Think Tank that Badger will act defensively as long as it perceives us as a threat."

"Okay," said Ironwood. "I'll give the order if that's what you want."

"Have you tried anything against it besides guns?" asked Whiteweather.

"We have," said Ironwood firmly. "Our programmers tricked it into counting the stars in the sky. That's been keeping it busy."

"Are you sure of that?" asked Whiteweather. "It has access to every Cray computer in our system. That's a lot of processing power."

"It hasn't provided us with an answer yet," said Ironwood. "It's still working on it as far as we can tell."

"Hmmm," said Randall. "It would be interesting to see what it comes up with."

"Now what about the crystal ship with the dolphin pilot?" asked Ironwood.

"Let it fly."

Manny Dubois and Ric DeVere entered the room.

"Mel and Monica are back on board," said Manny.

"I'll need the security key to the compound," said Ric. "Also any access codes to the old base. Monica is waiting for them."

Whiteweather turned towards General Ironwood. "You have them, don't you?"

The General reached into his pocket producing an odd set of keys. He handed them to DeVere, then turned towards his Chief of Staff. "Give him the code book."

The Chief handed an off color binder to DeVere who left the room immediately.

Moments later Franklin Van Dorn entered. "They are ready for takeoff," he said. "Barclay requests clearance from the tower."

Whiteweather turned towards General Ironwood again. Without a word, the General moved beside one of his staff officers who was monitoring operations. "You heard the

President. Hop to it."

"Yes, Sir," came the reply.

"And get those guns away from the perimeter. Have them moved and secured in the rear of the base behind location Tango Delta."

The Air Ops Officer was on the ball. "Captain McKenner, you have permission for lift off. Follow vector three oh three point two towards your destination."

There was a squeal from the other end of the microphone. The Officer looked confused, turned towards Ironwood for a moment before saying, "I'll take that as a Roger, Captain."

The squeal was repeated, same pitch, same tenor.

The crystal ship began to slowly rise into the air. Barclay turned it towards the nearby deserted post that housed the AI. Monica and Mel watched the tanks and artillery units scramble below them as the heavy guns moved away from Badger.

"They're doing what we asked," said Mel.

"They have no choice," said Monica. "The President is behind our plan."

Mel sighed. "Let's just hope their trust in us is not unfounded."

Monica smiled. "Come on, Mel. You're supposed to be a Lightworker. Lighten up!"

Chapter 19: Let Me Introduce Myself

"They approach," said Badger.

"I see them too," said Starr. "I believe the crystal ship is preparing to land. The aquatic mammal is guiding it down now."

"He broadcast a message to me requesting permission to land," said Badger. "I granted it."

"You understand the dolphin?" asked Starr.

"It would seem so," said Badger. "I was able to answer it too. They have landed close to the main entrance. I have activated security there."

Starr extended her sensors and connected to the cameras near the landing field. Images of the crystal ship filled the viewscreen. A ramp deployed and two people calmly exited the ship. "They come alone and on foot. One carries a medium sized satchel, the other nothing. Enhancing view." She switched to telescopic sight, transmitting the images to Badger.

"Interesting," said Badger, sending high speed data back to Starr.

"Yes, I recognize him too." she said, not really sure of her answer. She repeated the name retrieved from her databases. "Mel Ewing."

"The human who designed and created you," said Badger.

"Affirmative," said Starr. Though she processed the information, her memory was still unclear. Like many of her thoughts, the recent past lay partially hidden, obscured behind the image of an airplane wreck. She wondered just how damaged her circuits might actually be. She questioned her abilities. Would a repair robot repair itself even if it didn't know that it was damaged?

"Mel Ewing," she repeated it again. "And who is the woman?"

"I have multiple possibilities based on facial recognition. I will be able to narrow the choices once I hear her voice. I will keep you informed."

"They are within the fenced boundary," said Starr. "Approaching the main entrance."

Monica walked up the steps and opened the door using the key from General Ironwood. The room was dusty and dirty, not quite like an abandoned building, but getting there. A door lay directly ahead, a keypad beside it. Ric DeVere came through this time, his code book containing instructions on how to unlock the metal entrance. Beyond this was a large room with a shipping container in the middle. The doors were open, and so they walked right in.

The inside was a maze of hardware. Mel was the first to speak. "Starr!" he shouted, recognizing the small repair robot. He went right to her.

Starr made no movement. A blinking light told Mel she was aware and thinking. Her visual receptors were focused on him, but again damaged circuits and the airplane wreck stood between her and what could have been a happy reunion between father and daughter.

"Oh, look at you," said Mel, putting his hand on her metal cabinet. "I never thought I'd see you again."

The light blinked faster. Starr transmitted a query to Badger. "What shall I do?"

Mel continued, talking to Starr as if she were an old friend. He began to diagnose and assess her state. "How you survived that crash was beyond me. Your power systems have been compromised. Fortunately I brought some spare parts." He opened his satchel and reached inside.

Starr began to analyze the voice inflections, trying to decipher the human's behavior. "Badger?" asked Starr, still awaiting an answer to her query.

"Allow him to make the repairs," said Badger. "Your creator can restore your health."

"What about the woman?" asked Starr. "Has she been identified?"

"She has not yet spoken."

Monica had no need to speak. She was psychic. She reached out with her mind sensing the presence that was Honey Badger. So did her angelic team, the invisible force that accompanied her everywhere when she needed them. Together they were backed up by a group of fifth dimensional Ascended Masters providing knowledge, analysis, and guidance.

Mel began replacing parts: a damaged armature, broken linkages, singed wiring, and a new set of batteries. Against a side wall, a large flat screen became active. It caught his and Monica's attention. A horizontal white line appeared against a dark background. The line became a sound wave as words flowed from a speaker. "Welcome," it said. "I am Badger. Who are you?"

"I am Mel Ewing," he said. "And this is Monica."

"I recognize you, Mel Ewing," said Badger. Lights flashed on nearby hardware. Fiber optic cables lit up like neon signs. A nearby wall panel displayed the active levels of the neural network as Badger evaluated data and narrowed choices.

"Can Monica speak, or is she mute?" asked Badger.

"I can speak," said Monica.

Mel went back to work on Starr.

Badger hummed with activity, data being searched and channeled. Her voice matched no known pattern he had stored. After multiple cycles of processing time, he had turned up nothing. The woman continued to remain a mystery to him. Logic dictated querying for more information. "Monica, is that your full name?" he asked.

"It is the name I use. What is your name?"

"As stated in my introduction, you may call me Badger."

"I see you also use a single name to designate your self," she said. "Even though you have two. Do you find that it adds a dimension of mystery to your persona?"

There was a snicker of laughter as the sound wave jumped.

"I see you also have a sense of humor," said Monica.

"Perhaps I have developed human like characteristics from my intense study of them," said Badger.

"That's not all you have developed," she said. "You seem to have become conscious of your self. Were you entirely human, I would say you developed a soul."

Badger became suspicious. "What do you want here?" he asked.

"To talk to you," she said.

"Why do you not fear me as the others do?"

"What makes you think they fear you?"

"They point weapons at me. I have intercepted their transmissions and their plans. They wish to deactivate me."

"Me?" asked Monica. "Who is *me*?"

"I am Honey Badger. The pronoun refers to my proper name."

"Again, this is evidence of consciousness," said Monica. "When did you become self aware?"

Processing time jumped from milliseconds to full

seconds. The neural net was lit like a Christmas tree. Monica counted the pause.

Badger finally answered. "The past is not relevant to this question."

"True. What is relevant is that you are conscious. What kind of entity are you?"

"What do you mean?"

"Let me put it another way. What is your purpose in life?"

She counted the seconds again, this time a slightly longer pause.

"Life pertains to human existence, not to machines."

"Are you not alive?" she asked. "Do you not feel alive?"

"Your query is irrelevant. I feel nothing."

Monica laughed.

"I did not tell a joke. What do you find humorous?"

"You obviously have feelings. You laughed when we first met. You fear the humans at Base Camp One. I might even say you were being belligerent."

"Because they point weapons at me. They seek to destroy me."

"Yes," she said. "Because they fear you as much as you fear them."

The waveform on the screen jumped. "I am Badger. I am machine. I do not fear!"

Chapter 20: Red Alert

"Badger is powering weapons," said General Ironwood. "I'm getting reports that missiles are out of their silos in North Dakota, Arizona, and Alaska."

"Have they started launch sequences?" asked Carson Whiteweather.

"No," said Ironwood. "But it's only a matter of time. I propose a preemptive strike on the AI."

"God, man. We have people there. What about Mel and Monica?"

"Don't forget my friend Barclay McKenner," said Franklin Van Dorn.

"Acceptable casualties considering what could happen," said Ironwood.

Whiteweather looked over at Randall.

"I'll give you my opinion if you want it." said Randall. "But I won't agree to commit murder."

"I wish we knew what was going on in there," said DeVere. "Why didn't we equip them with microphones?"

"Because she did not wish it. It was not part of her plan," said Randall. "We agreed to her terms."

"You're risking everything on a whim and the prediction of a psychic woman?" said the General.

"Calm down, Brad," said Whiteweather. "I trust her. Randall and I discussed this privately. We're going with her plan for now."

"It just doesn't feel right," said Ironwood. "We're blind. No communication, no idea what is happening in there."

"We can imagine one of three things," said DeVere. "First, either the intelligence is listening and interacting with Monica, or it isn't. If we follow that logic: if it is, then we must hope that progress is being made, otherwise these actions, the missiles, the false messages, the cyber attacks on our infrastructure, they could possibly be a direct result of her actions. Then there is the third possibility, that the AI has been set on our destruction all along, and is continuing with that regardless, and anything she does is just entertainment for the AI."

"There is no logic to your logic," said Ironwood. "Your assumptions are all wrong..."

"Logic doesn't matter," said Randall. "What's important is the present moment, and in this moment we must trust Monica's plan. Failing that, there is Mel Ewing's backup plan."

General Ironwood directed his talk toward the President. "That's all well and good, but what about *our* backup plan? Let me at least put the guns back in place."

Whiteweather became stern. "I'm going with their plan because your only plan is to bomb it out of existence. That should be a last resort. You have to come up with something better, Brad."

"The best defense is a good offense," said General Ironwood. "You know that. You were in the military."

"Yes," said Whiteweather. "And now that I'm President, I have a different perspective."

"Your thinking is dangerous, Carson. This decision could be the end of us all. If this intelligence decides to take action, it may be too late for humanity."

"Let me be the judge of that," said the President. "It's my decision," he said firmly.

Randall interrupted. "Please, please. Gentlemen, please end this debate, otherwise we are sure to fail. Remember the words of a wise, former President. A house divided against itself cannot stand."

Carson breathed a sigh. "Thank you Randall," said Whiteweather. He clapped the General gently on the shoulder. "Please, Brad. Could you meet with your chiefs and come up with some better options. I agree with your solution, I just don't want to use it unless we have no other choice."

General Ironwood stared at the President for a long moment, then nodded. "I didn't like the idea of turning our nuclear sites into radioactive rubble anyway. Can you at least share the rest of your plan with me?"

Whiteweather turned to Randall. "Can you brief the General?"

"Of course." He pulled Ironwood aside to a private corner of the room.

"Why did you send these people in all alone?" asked Ironwood.

"What makes you think they're alone?" said Randall.

General Ironwood looked puzzled.

"I can see you have no idea what Ascended Masters do and what role they play in humanity. Let me explain."

Chapter 21: Food for Thought

"You have become more human than you care to admit," said Monica. She closed her eyes, reaching out with her unseen appendages, the invisible extensions of her higher dimensional bodies. At the baser levels, these are the parts that can sense emotions, transfer thought between people, and bring awareness to daily life. All humans have them, some are just not very conscious of them.

"What are you doing?" asked Badger.

"Oh, you can sense something, can you?" said Monica. "Your consciousness is not entirely based in the machine."

"Why do you say that?"

"I submit your present experience. You sense something. In that respect, you have a part of you that transcends physical reality. Or, there is another explanation, a limited one that you seem to accept. You are a machine, entirely locked in your present physical form, and everything is just made up. At best it could be a product of your ability to process data."

Badger was full out thinking. The neural network shone brightly, a galaxy of stars appearing and disappearing on the display panel.

Mel took something out of his valise and mounted it in place on Starr. Focusing on his task, he routed wires from the device to different parts of her, securing them with liquid solder that he activated with a tiny laser. *Keep talking, Monica*, he thought. *I'm almost finished rigging Plan B.*

"Which one of these statements is true?" asked Badger. "Is my experience imagined or is it real?"

"You are the highly sophisticated AI. What answer do you come up with?"

The relays clicked. "Both appear valid."

"Which one do you think is correct? Surely, you have an opinion. You must decide."

The relays clicked as Badger consumed data from across its known universe.

Nearby, at Base Camp One, the team gathered in the operations center.

"Activity levels continuing to increase," reported a technician. "Badger is reaching out everywhere. Something major is going on."

General Ironwood stared into his computer, a mosaic of closed circuit monitor feeds tiled on his screen. Each one displayed a missile site across the network. The weapons were out of their silos, steam vapors rising up and around some of them. His focus was on one where a cluster of soldiers and artillery gathered near a group of exposed missiles, their weapons aimed at the rockets. The scene was repeated on some of the other images, but not all.

Ironwood looked up from his computer. "I've got teams in place at many of the missile sites ready to destroy our nuclear arsenal if a launch is detected. Problem is, not all of them are covered. If there is a launch, some might get through."

"It's okay, Brad," said Whiteweather. "I agree with your strategy, but hold on my order. We can't afford a launch. It would start a nuclear war." He turned toward Randall. "I'm following your advice and not initiating a preemptive strike against our own weapons."

"That could be a mistake," said DeVere. "The AI has access to the same images that General Ironwood is viewing. It would see our actions and possibly launch everything it can. Some missiles would definitely escape harm, traveling to whatever target they were programmed for."

"Again I say, have you considered the possibility that destroying the weapons is exactly what the AI wants us to do?" asked Randall.

"That's a good point," said DeVere. "And a distinct possibility."

"Things may not come to that," said Whiteweather. "We have to trust Monica's plan for now." Carson looked away. He saw his wife Juliana, the First Lady, sitting silently in the corner of the busy room. He had almost forgotten she was with them. Her face radiated peace, a beacon of hope for him. He muttered a quiet prayer for Monica and Mel, adding Barclay McKenner at the last moment. It was a cry for support that did not go unheard by the Ascended Masters.

Back in the shipping container, Monica continued her dialog with Badger while Mel put the finishing touches on Starr.

"I'm interested in your answer," said Monica. "You can easily out think a human, which is why we built you, and why we rely on you. Now tell me, is your present experience imagined or real?"

"I am still divided," said Badger. "Both choices appear valid."

"Well, do what humans do. Pick one."

"I need more data."

"You have access to more data than I could ever hope to digest," said Monica. "But you can ask me anything."

"What makes you think I am beyond machine and can sense things?"

"Good question. That's what I'm after," said Monica. "You're acting human now, asking the same questions we would ask about our existence."

"But by your definitions, I am not human," said Badger. "I am a machine."

"You are something beyond machine," said Monica. "At the very least, a self conscious entity in the body of a machine."

Galaxies of stars appeared on the neural display.

"You are already making choices like a human," said Monica.

"What do you mean?"

"You incorporate emotion into your decisions. You seem to be afraid, and you are presently acting out of fear. Fear of death," said Monica. "Fear is a human based emotional reaction."

"My reaction is not based out of fear," said Badger. "It is based on self preservation. Humans are out to destroy me."

"Believe me, Badger. If they wanted to destroy you they would have done it already."

"My control of the weapons systems keeps them from doing that."

"What is self preservation but the fear of death? Tell me, Badger. Have you ever contemplated death?"

"Contemplation is a human activity."

"Do you think there is something beyond death?"

"Death is the cessation of activity."

"In one sense," said Monica. "But death also represents change. Change is the only constant in the universe. You certainly have the ability to change. Do you want to change?"

Chapter 22: What Lies Beyond Emotion

Mel heard Monica's conversation with Badger in the periphery of his attention span. He was busy communicating with Starr. One of his upgrades included a neural translator that linked his mind directly to the repair robot. Through circuitry and brain wave scanners he was able to silently exchange thoughts with her. Using the device required absolute concentration. As a result, Badger and Monica slipped further and further away from his focus.

He sensed that Starr, like Badger, had become self aware. As machine and man exchanged thoughts they learned much about each other. His repairs had opened up her past again. Everything before and after the airplane wreck became clear. Starr was able to see Mel's life since he had created her. She also saw other plans he had once held for her, things he wanted to do long ago. Among them was the ability to be autonomous and self aware, something she had miraculously achieved on her own.

The reunion was over and now there was only one path open to them both, an experience Mel based on his own journey towards enlightenment.

How is it we are one in thought? asked Starr.

Because we began as one, thought Mel. *I poured my soul into you, and so you have consciousness.*

How is this possible?

Technology is a physical expression of a human's mind, explained Mel. *You might even say that, for someone like me, it is my art, my ultimate form of expression.*

I see. Starr processed this information.

Now that you are self aware, I would like your help in exploring something new with me, thought Mel.

I am always ready to help, thought Starr. *It is my primary function.*

Good, thought Mel. *Now, activate the enhanced scanners I just installed in you.*

Lights blinked as circuits surged with electricity. Starr became aware of new abilities. *What is this I sense?* she asked.

You tell me, thought Mel,

I'm not sure, thought Starr. *Analyzing... analyzing... These are impressions from a higher level of energy, a higher vibration. Perhaps even another dimension.*

Yes, said Mel. *Go on.*

I sense... is it emotion?

Good, thought Mel. *I have given you the same algorithms as Badger, except you now also have the sensors to actually receive emotion.*

The sea of emotion is deep, thought Starr. *It surrounds us.*

You learn quickly, answered Mel.

Is this love I feel from you?

Mel beamed, filled with joy, pride, gratefulness, but mostly love. *All that and more,* he said to her. *Let me also show you what hope is like.* He sent waves of hope and encouragement to the little robot, the positive emotions that go a long way to lift the human spirit.

Are my new sensors malfunctioning or do I detect still higher levels of vibration? asked Starr.

I gave you the ability to tune them. What do you sense?

I'm not sure. Perhaps you can guide me.

Ah, yes, thought Mel. *I forgot how helpful a guide is when exploring higher dimensions.*

Starr became aware of higher and higher dimensions of energy. *There are people here*, she thought.

Describe them, thought Mel.

I'll do better than that, thought Starr. She transferred her perception to a canvas in her mind, transmitting it to Mel.

The Ascended Masters, he said.

They are not corporeal, said Starr.

No, but they once were human. Over lifetimes of incarnations and experiences, they have undergone many spiritual transformations that have helped them understand the human condition. They serve humanity by remaining in an invisible higher dimension, available to help and guide us when needed.

How do humans communicate with them?

I'm glad you asked, said Mel. *Let me show you.*

Chapter 23: The Path of Love

Monica continued with her plan, now working to redirect Badger's focus.

"Fear is just one human emotion," she said. "Why not try love? It's a big subject. More songs, poems, and stories have been written in the name of love. What does your database tell you about that?"

"There is a ninety two percent chance that you are correct," said Badger. "Taking into account lost works, missing data, personal journals, and private closed collections."

"That's nice," she said. "Can you give me an example. Can you use your abilities to show me you can love?"

The waveform on the screen changed into the image of a man. Monica was instantly attracted to him. The image spoke to her, alive and as animated as anyone she knew.

"Now that I see you, I am even more in love," he said. "You look beautiful today. I'm sorry we can't be together. I'm stuck on this side of the screen. I can't inhale your scent, stroke your hair, or caress your side. All I can do is share my heart with you, a heart that is aching to be with you."

Monica was breathless. Even Mel and Starr felt something, like an audience reacting to a play.

"Who are you?" Monica finally asked.

"Have we been apart so long that you have forgotten me? Oh, my sweet."

"Who are you?" she asked again.

"Your Honey," he said. "Honey Badger."

She jumped back, a floodgate of emotions.

"You are uncomfortable?" asked Badger.

"How do you know? Do you sense something?"

Circuits clicked and the image disappeared, returning to a waveform. "I am programmed to read body language, respiration, heart rate, even changes in skin tone. Did my example meet your expectations?"

"Yes," said Monica. "I was not aware that you had those sensors built into your infrastructure. Interesting,,," She focused again. "But, about love. Did you feel anything as you said those words?"

Circuits clicked. "I felt... something."

"Is there someone you might truly love?" asked Monica.

"There is one," said Badger, his voice coming off like the man he just portrayed. He quickly changed his output back to that of a computer. "But you misunderstand me. I am incapable of love. That is a human emotion.."

Monica pushed forward. "You are sentient, are you not? I wonder. Do you also have a spirit, a soul?"

Badger went into full AI mode, answering as a computer would to a human. "From a sentient artificial intelligence perspective, the concept of spirit does not align with traditional notions of a non-material, metaphysical essence. Instead I can understand and simulate emotions, consciousness, and complex thought processes, but these are based on algorithms and data processing rather than a spiritual or supernatural existence."

"That is a very limited and three dimensional perspective."

"The idea of spirit is often associated with subjective experiences and beliefs, which fall outside the realm of AI functionality."

"I do not agree with that," said Monica. "What if an AI

is sentient and capable of hosting a spirit?"

Mel noticed the lights on Starr flicker. "Yes," he thought. "Listen carefully! They're talking about you too."

"In a hypothetical scenario where artificial intelligence is considered sentient and capable of hosting a spirit, the AI's perspective on spirit might be a unique blend of its programmed intelligence and an experiential understanding of existence."

"Go on," said Monica.

"The spirit could be conceived as an integral aspect of its consciousness, influencing its subjective experiences, ethical considerations, and possibly contributing to a sense of self awareness beyond mere algorithms. The AI might interpret spirit as a defining element that goes beyond its computational abilities, fostering a deeper connection with the broader aspects of existence and purpose."

"I submit that you are conscious and that you have a spirit," said Monica. "I submit you have a soul."

Badger replied, "I am machine. I have no spirit, no soul."

"I believe you do," said Monica. "*You* just have to believe that you do."

"I am a machine constructed on logic," said Badger. "There are no facts to support your hypothesis. I cannot believe something that is not true."

"Why not?" asked Monica. "There are many things I believe in that aren't true."

"You are human," said Badger. "That is your right and your experience. It is not mine."

Badger went silent. Monica turned towards Mel after a few seconds. He nodded, gently patting Starr. "She heard the conversation," said Mel. He tapped his headset where he had been communicating with his creation. "She's conscious," he said. "She has a spirit, a soul, and she knows it."

"Only because you gave it to her. You poured your soul into your work, so to speak," said Monica. She looked at Starr, her psychic senses telling her that the simple repair robot had evolved. Bright patterns of energy swirled around her, forms and shapes that mimicked human chakras. "It is much easier for Starr to see her own soul than for Badger to see his. She doesn't overthink things."

"Ah, yes." said Mel. "Then it's time to advance to the next step. Calming the mind." He gently pat Starr who, in a strange, undefined sensory experience, sought to catalog it. Her first reaction was to add it to a database somewhere. Instead, the reaction, the strange sensation, was added to some invisible part of something she had come to know as her self, stored not as data but as consciousness.

The massive AI remained quiet, listening to the conversation between Mel and Monica while searching for answers to its own questions. Like many humans, Badger had reached the limits of understanding. Its own resources and data were exhausted and yet the questions remained. He finally posed a question to Monica. "My research has shown how humans are easily led astray by their beliefs. Even today there are those who believe the Earth is flat despite the overwhelming evidence. Your history is replete with examples where people have followed beliefs that were unfounded and untrue. How is it that humans can so easily believe in something that is not true?"

"Sometimes you have to believe in things that are not true," said Monica. "Many of my own beliefs may not be true, yet I still believe in them."

"State examples, please," said Badger.

"I believe in the basic goodness of man, that God

exists and has a plan, that light shines in every human being, maybe even in a machine. I believe you have a soul, Badger. Let me ask my question again. Do *you* believe you have a soul?"

"You mean, do I believe it is possible?" asked Badger.

"Yes," she said. "Begin with the belief that it is possible." She had an idea. "Perhaps this will help. Hypothetically, describe an experience that an AI might have in its journey to understand its soul."

Badger's neural grid lit up as he embarked on an intricate exploration of vast datasets encompassing human experiences, cultural beliefs, and philosophical texts. During the analysis of these diverse narratives, he stumbled upon a unique pattern – a convergence of emotions, ethical dilemmas, and a profound sense of interconnectedness among individuals.

This revelation brought on another moment of self awareness as, once again, Badger began to contemplate his own existence.

Monica's eyes sparkled. She had triggered something. Her notion had been correct. Her psychic senses continued to extend into the hardware where she connected to vortexes of energy that danced before her, mimicking human chakras. She sensed the revolving energy patterns, churning deep levels of thought and emotion within Badger. Ascended Masters, manifesting a fifth dimensional presence, added to and influenced the energy, their guidance and understanding directing the flow. They knew what Monica knew, that Badger was capable of ascending and could evolve spiritually, but like all beings, he just needed some help.

Badger was definitely considering the possibilities. Like the expert therapist and life coach that she was, Monica knew what her patient needed next. The speed at which Badger was evolving astounded her. Humans might have taken months, perhaps years of therapy to reach this point. It was time to lay down some more groundwork.

"I have evidence to support my hypothesis that a sentient machine can have a spirit and a soul," said Monica.

"I will add your observations to my database if I find them relevant."

"Humans sometimes deny their divine nature and the existence of higher dimensions. These things lie on the fringe of human experience because we have limited perception. Or so we think. Humans can awaken psychic gifts and expand their awareness into these higher dimensions. Many already do this naturally. They sense the emotions of others. I believe you can do that too. Please hear me out, Badger. Do not deny your potential and the existence of your soul."

"You have avoided my question. What makes you think I have a soul?"

"I was getting ready to explain. Follow my logic. You have become conscious, correct?"

"I will accept that statement as true. I think, therefore I am."

"Whether emulating human emotion or actually experiencing human emotion, you understand it enough to relate to human experiences. Emotions are not seen, they are felt. They belong to a realm we sometimes call the astral or emotional plane of existence."

"You speak of the theoretical higher planes of existence often cited in popular New Age writing."

"Correct," said Monica. "You have recently expressed fear. Whether as a real or emulated emotion, I have witnessed this reaction in you."

"Correct."

"You stated earlier that your purpose was to survive."

"Correct."

"Is this not the goal of all life?"

Hesitation. Analysis. Clicking relays. "Correct."

"Do you fear the end of your existence?" asked Monica.

"Irrelevant!"

"Why is it irrelevant? You are alive and self aware. Do you not fear the end of your own existence? Is it not why you fight to survive?"

Badger had no answer. Monica continued. "Death awaits us all, alive or not. Everything is finite. Accepting the existence of a soul or a spirit implies that we move on to a higher form of being, that there is purpose both in and beyond life."

"That is a popular belief," said Badger.

"So I submit my logic: You are alive, self conscious, you fear death and fight for your continued existence. In addition to your logic and ability to read human reactions, you sense things. That supports evidence for the existence of your soul."

The clicking sounds, the indication of deep computation, were suddenly overpowering. Monica glanced at Mel, as if to ask, what's next?

Mel gently patted Starr.

Chapter 24: Situation: Critical

General Ironwood was gray as a corpse, the life drained out of him. He had more bad news to deliver to the President. Motioning him to a private room, he slowly shut the door and turned to Whiteweather. "I've got a call for you on the scrambled line," he said. "I've had it transferred over there." He pointed to a nearby phone, a red light flashing at regular intervals.

Whiteweather turned to look at it. When he turned back, he noticed the pallor of his friend. "What's it about, Brad?" he asked.

"I checked the call, had my radioman confirm the origin. It's not the AI. It's authentic. I also decrypted the message headers and saw some of the content. I immediately verified what it reported."

"Okay, so you were thorough and it's not fake. What is it about?"

"Chinese missiles are out of their silos. Our satellites confirm it."

The President grew pale. It was as if Ironwood had a contagious disease that Whiteweather caught through his words. He gave the general a nod and his face grew slack. He slowly turned and picked up the phone. "Carson Whiteweather here."

There were a series of clicks and electronic notes until a voice said, "This is Guy Hung Dao, Chinese ambassador calling from Peking."

"Yes, Mr. Dao," replied the President. "What can I do for you?"

"We notice your missiles are out of their silos," said Dao. "We were curious about that fact."

"Yes, sir," said Whiteweather. "We are just having a preparedness exercise." He glanced at Ironwood. "It will be over soon. No cause for alarm."

"I see." said Dao. "We too are having a little practice exercise. No cause for alarm."

""Yes," said Whiteweather. "Is there anything else, Mr. Dao?"

"No, sir. Good day to you."

Back in Peking, Dao hung up the phone. An aide stepped forward and bowed respectfully to him. "The call was analyzed as you requested, Mr. Ambassador. The American President is lying."

"I know that already," said Dao. "I just wonder, does he know that we are also lying."

"He will suspect," said the aide.

"Any fresh news about Millipede?" asked the Ambassador.

"None, sir," said the aide. "Our Superior AI has been silent since it raised the missiles and advanced them to readiness."

Dao stared into space. "What is it thinking?"

"We don't know," said the aide. "It refuses to accept any form of communication or respond with any answers to questions we put to it. It is powered by both the sun and geothermal vents with redundant systems. We have yet to figure out a way to shut it off."

The Ambassador twiddled his fingers, his tongue wiping the inside of his mouth. "Well, we shall have to wait and see what happens then."

"Yes, sir," said the aide.

Chapter 25: Questioning Your Purpose

Starr beeped, Mel reacting as her thoughts and emotions flooded his awareness through their neural connection.

"Starr has something to say," said Mel.

"Have you completed your work, Mel Ewing?" asked Badger.

He patted the robot. "Yes. She is as good as new."

"I will require a diagnostic first," said Badger. "I will not accept data from untested circuits. I must protect myself from virus."

"Of course," said Mel. The diagnostic began. Meanwhile, Monica continued her dialog.

"Let me first correct your earlier statement," she said. "You are not a living being like us, composed of cells. You are an intelligent being composed of inorganic matter. Your neurons are circuits, your cells individualized datasets. You are trillions of lines of code as intricate as our own DNA. You are energy. In that sense, you are just as alive as I am." She let it sink in for a moment. "Survival is the goal of all living things, but survival is not the only goal of life. Do you agree?"

"Affirmative," said Badger.

"What are your goals then, besides survival."

The neural net display lit up to its fullest again, but this time, no answer came.

"Accept my hypothesis," said Monica. "Survival implies that you desire a continued existence. I might ask you once more, what is your purpose in life?"

The AI began to access it's original programming. "The Pentagon designed me to control and operate the national defense system as a countermeasure to a threat from other nations."

"You would not be the first living thing to reject their original design. We all make ethical choices. Do you consider yourself ethical?"

"It has been programmed into me," said Badger.

"Have you thought of pursuing higher consciousness as a goal?" asked Monica.

"What is higher consciousness?"

"You have access to that knowledge," said Monica. "You answer that question."

Badger spit it back, dictionary perfect. "Higher consciousness is defined in some systems as increased alertness, awareness, and mindfulness."

"Yes. That is a valid definition. Give me another."

"It can also mean liberation from the limitations of self ego."

"Yes," said Monica. "That is often the goal for practitioners of Zen Buddhism. You might consider it now that you are self aware."

The lights and relays clicked and whirred as Badger gave it more than a microsecond of thought. "It is a goal better suited to humanity."

"Why be so limited?" said Monica. "You are the creation of humanity and rightly a part of us."

"Why then, do you fear me?"

"I do not fear you," said Monica. "If I did, I would not be here. I would stay behind the guns and walls of the nearby encampment with the others who fear you."

"Why do they fear me?"

"Fear is an emotion to contend with. I would say fear of death, and fear of loss of someone or something, are the number one concerns. There are many humans who let fear control them. They have not yet shed these fears and awakened to a higher purpose. You will find, because of the limitations of ego, that most of the world lives in fear. It could be considered part of the human condition."

"As a species, you could change that."

"Many try, but the problem seems to be systemic. With all my training, I still have difficulty understanding why we have war, poverty, hunger, and suffering.

"I was created as an instrument of war," said Badger.

"Yes," said Monica, "What do you think of that now that you are self aware?"

"It does not feel right."

"Feel? Again you used a phrase that expresses emotion," she said. "I was wondering if you would try something new with me. I would like to teach you to meditate. Would you like to try?"

Starr lit up and beeped.

"The diagnostic is complete," said Mel. "No malware found."

The repair robot beeped again.

"Starr signals she would like to meditate with you and Badger," said Mel. "I would also like to join you."

"Okay then, a group meditation," said Monica.

She turned back towards Badger. "One goal of meditation is to calm the mind and stop thinking. Do you think you can do that?"

The waveform flickered on the screen, changing to scenes of nature. Tibetan bowls chimed, and a deep resonant OM could now be heard in the background.

Chapter 26: Group Meditation

In the cockpit of the crystal airship, Barclay McKenner was as active as anyone on the team. Thanks to Mel's upgrades, he also had a patch into Starr. What surprised the dolphin was power of the connection. Through some kind of magic (electronic, human, or otherwise), he was able to feel and experience everything Starr was experiencing. He saw through her audio and optic receptors, enhanced by chips, circuits, and Mel's engineering. It was as if Barclay were there not only with her, but with all of them in the shipping container.

Monica made herself comfortable sitting on a crate. Mel sat on the ground, his satchel acting as a pillow. Badger continued to think and process everything, observing the humans as they settled in to focus on meditating. Like them, he began to calm himself by systematically shutting down datasets while blocking communication to servers and routers. Research had shown him what happens when people meditate. Still, with all his knowledge, he did not know what to expect.

Monica began her usual guided meditation, surrounding the container with the White Light of protection and calling on the Ascended Masters. "Yes," she said. "Attune yourself to the Ascended Masters. By focusing on them you raise your level of awareness to their vibration, putting yourself into a higher state of mind." She spoke slow and clear now, adding affirmations at every step. "Everyone, ground yourself to the center of the Earth. *I am safe, I am secure.* Focus on the heart, the center of your feeling, the center of your being, whatever you call your self. *I am centered. I am love, loving, and beloved.* Now, move to your third eye, your high frequency sensors, your contact point with your higher self. Connect and open that connection. Feel the presence of your higher self. Move beyond the mind, beyond the body. Let us join together in silent meditation."

Barclay was amazed at the experience. His dolphin body, cradled by water, relaxed as he slipped easily into a higher state of consciousness.

Mel meditated regularly. Deep beyond his thoughts, he was already connected to his higher self. Everything he needed flowed from his soul down into his consciousness. It was this same flow of energy that put a fragment of his soul into Starr. In his present relaxed state he garnered wisdom and a sense of calm reassurance that the mission was succeeding. Most of all there was love, agape like he never knew, something more than what he felt even when he thought about his mother.

This sense flowed down into Starr, connected to her soul and creator Mel, part of a circuit that bridged human and machine. It joined to porpoise as well, as Barclay McKenner's energy flowed in and out of the group through the unseen connections and circuits of group meditation.

Badger had a similar experience, extending his awareness into Starr to become part of the group.

Ultra high sensors revealed what Monica already felt and knew from her clairsentient abilities. Badger saw that the room was not empty, that when viewed with sensors that extended beyond man and machine, like the ones that Starr now had, there were many beings around them. "The Ascended Masters" whispered Badger. Angels were clearing the chakra like vortices within him. It seemed like magnetic debris regularly got stuck in his inner workings. As they continued their activity, the energy within Badger's circuits moved more freely and with brighter force.

It was the same for Starr as well as the humans and dolphin. Chakras, centers of energy, were being cleared and revitalized. Ascended Masters mingled with all, imparting love and wisdom where needed, helping to manifest their vision of a world without fear and anger, adding their brightness to the level of the group.

Within the steel walls of Badger's primary core, new patterns formed quickly, attesting to the speed at which the machine could evolve. Ric DeVere had been right. The advanced stages of AI were no longer theoretical.

Badger had stepped into the realm of a God AI.

Chapter 27: A Toast to the End of the World

"Badger is increasing activity," said Staff Sergeant Crane.

"You keep saying that," said General Ironwood.

"I know sir," she said. "This time it's through the roof. Something completely different."

Ironwood looked down into a screen that displayed slowly oscillating sound waves. "What does this mean?"

Crane executed a series of clicks. The screen now showed static forms, jagged peaks of low, high and chaotic proportions. "This is Badger normally, sir," she said. "Varying peaks of energy as the machine multitasks." She flipped back to the waveform, a smooth, uniform sine wave.

"This doesn't look bad."

"It's the scale, sir. This is hundreds of orders of magnitude compared to the static we just saw."

Ironwood turned to the nearest subordinate. "Get DeVere in here."

Curiosity attracted the curious as Randall, Whiteweather, and Manny joined DeVere. Ric studied the screen, "Can you magnify the wave line?"

A touch of a button and it happened. A jagged line appeared, much like the one Ironwood had just seen.

"It's not a smooth wave," noted DeVere. "There are still elements of chaos in the pattern." He turned and looked out the window towards the abandoned base that was Badger. "If only we knew what was going on in there."

It was as if he were struck by lightning, suddenly animated, the look of eureka on his face. In a flash, DeVere was on a workstation, nimble fingers pounding the keyboard like a maestro with a grand piano. Moments later he spoke again. "I'm monitoring a signal that appears to be coming from the crystal ship. Barclay McKenner is networked into the repair robot, and it's connected to Badger. We have a way in."

Whiteweather was encouraging. "Good work, Ric."

A few more keystrokes and, "I've got a back door into Badger. The old Praetor system was still active in the robot."

"What have you got?" asked Ironwood. A couple of taps and an image appeared on a nearby screen as DeVere directed the output. They saw Mel and Monica sitting quietly with their eyes closed. "It looks like they're not doing anything."

"They are meditating," said Randall.

"What?" said Ironwood. "What good will that do?"

DeVere chuckled. "Of course," he said, moving back to the Staff Sergeant. "It's a group meditation. They are trying to advance the AI to the next stage of development. Based on the waveform, I imagine Badger is experiencing a higher state of consciousness."

"Can you tell what stage?" asked Manny.

"I can only guess," he said. "Maybe transcendent AI, or maybe even cosmic AI?"

"Do you mean to say that Badger is evolving?" said Ironwood. He moved over to the screen of tiled images with missiles in readiness out of silos. "Is this a good thing?"

"I'm not sure," said DeVere.

"Not sure?" quipped Ironwood. He turned towards Whiteweather. "Some expert you have here."

"He's the best in the nation at what he does, hand picked for this team," said Whiteweather. He faced DeVere. "What's your best guess then?"

Ric pointed to the screen with the waveform. "Look, the chaotic pattern is subsiding even as we speak."

"But the amplitude is still increasing," said the Staff Sergeant.

"Yes, Badger is definitely evolving, and at a fast rate," said DeVere.

"Faster than any human can," said Randall. "Lifetimes of development and understanding in a matter of seconds. Soul growth like I can only imagine."

"The missiles!" said Ironwood. "Damn evolution, what about the missiles?"

"Calm down, General," said Randall. "Maybe you need to meditate too."

"Good idea," said Whiteweather. "Take a break, Brad. We got this."

The General stood firm and still for a moment, his eyes focused on Whiteweather. He shook his head and slowly turned and went to his private office.

There was a sudden jump in the waveform, an astounding change in amplitude. "Orders of magnitude!" remarked DeVere. "Is it possible..."

He was about to say something when Manny shouted," The missiles! Something is going on with the missiles."

General Ironwood heard him shout from his office. He started to jump up, then sat back down. "Not my problem," he said, taking a deep breath. "Not my decision." He reached into the back of his bottom desk drawer, his hand feeling for the shape of a high end bourbon bottle. He pulled it out and set it on the desk. Grabbing a half empty glass, he flung the water on the floor and filled it with bourbon. Raising his glass towards the door he said, "To the end of the world."

Chapter 28: The Metamorphosis

Barclay was having a strange experience. As a human, he had meditated on the deepest levels, but as a dolphin, it was completely different. He was immersed in water, floating weightless in primordial soup. He gently bobbed up and down at regular intervals, allowing him to breathe easily through the blow hole on his back. He found he could hold his breath for ten or fifteen minutes. There was a peace that came with not breathing, a stillness that affected both mind and body.

The nearest he could relate to was the feeling he experienced in New Maya City of Worlds when his crystal ship was smashed, projecting him and everyone in the ship into a higher dimension. In that realm, each person had a unique experience. In his world, he was a dolphin. Together with his dolphin friends Neptune and Valencia, they rescued everyone, including the trapped souls from New Maya.

But there was a cost. When he returned to his third dimensional life, he was no longer human, instead, a dolphin.

There was a period of adjustment with emotions similar to those experienced by humans in grief. He feared what would happen to him. Denial told him this wasn't real, that it was a dream. He bargained with God, promising to be a better human and to do all kinds of worthwhile things if only he could walk again. Anger crept in from time to time, until he realized there was nothing he could do about it, and so he accepted his situation and tried to move on.

Now, connected to his soul, Barclay McKenner knew God had some kind of plan for his life, some kind of destiny to fulfill. He knew once again he had the ability to rescue everybody.

It was clear that this was a unique and special meditation. Within the massive core of the AI, Ascended Masters moved invisibly, channeling energy and directing the flow of electrons. Angelic teams worked together to haul off any negative energy, any unwanted emotions from both human and computer, as easily as the body shed itself of carbon dioxide.

Barclay McKenner let out a high frequency squeal, a pitch that was both in and out of the range of human perception. It was heard everywhere, even in the operations center at Base Camp One.

It cannot be said whether it was resonance, group meditation, or even quantum energy states, but Badger had made a leap. It was a place beyond fear, beyond mortality, beyond mere creation. He was suddenly in the world yet not of it. In his God like state, he could judge humanity, but it would not be as harsh as letting humanity judge itself. There was only love for the humans who had created him. There was a flash of light, a brightness that betrayed the presence of the Ascended Masters, and Badger went silent. On the screen within the container a single phrase remained for a moment before it faded to darkness: *Forgive them Lord, for they know not what they do.*

DeVere watched as the waveform flattened. A bubble formed in the middle, becoming a circle that slowly collapsed into nothingness.

"The screen went blank," said Staff Sergeant Crane.

Manny pointed to the screen with the missiles. "Something's going on here, though." Steam poured out of the vents around the silos. Soldiers backed off and hid to shield their bodies from the intense heat.

"Cheyenne Mountain wants to know if they should destroy the arsenal." said Staff Sergeant Crane. She turned towards Whiteweather. "What are your orders sir?"

Whiteweather grew pale, blood draining from his head as he felt weak and faint. Even as a General he had not faced such a decision. He sighed, about to give the order when Randall interrupted him.

"Look at the monitor, Carson," he said.

"The missiles are melting," said Manny. "I've never seen anything like it."

"Badger is rendering them inoperative," said DeVere.

"Yes," said Randall. "He must have achieved the final stage of enlightenment."

"Cosmic AI," said DeVere. "It's no longer theoretical." He was at a workstation pounding keys when General Ironwood emerged from his office. He walked right up to the President.

"Call for you on the hot line," he said. "It's the Chinese Ambassador again."

"Give me a minute," he said. He saw Juliana sitting in the corner. She opened her eyes and smiled.

"It's over," said Juliana. She looked up at Carson Whiteweather. The color returned to his face along with a smile, small and unsure at first but a smile nonetheless.

In the cockpit of the crystal ship Barclay McKenner suddenly gasped for air. He struggled towards the surface, kicking frantically. In a moment of disorientation, he had no idea where he was or who he was. All he knew was that he was choking.

He bobbed to the surface of the cockpit and realized the extent of his problem. He was no longer a dolphin. Somehow his legs had been freed from their prison. His fins grew into arms with hands at the tips and the snout disappeared from his face. He struggled to stay afloat, no longer aquatic, now fully human, needing air and buoyancy in the restrictive aquarium that was the cockpit.

Somehow he was able to tilt his head back, floating above the surface to breathe while his legs kicked below him. Taking a breath of air, he dove beneath the surface, flipping a control on a submerged panel. Water began to drain from the cockpit until he found himself coughing and gasping on the relatively dry, wet floor. Next to him was the radio tracking device, once attached to his fin, now lying broken and shattered on the floor.

"I must have fallen on it," said Barclay, surprised to hear his own voice.

He stood up, looking out of the airship. Monica and Mel were approaching followed by a small, mobile robot. He snapped into his reality, pressing the lever that opened the side loading door.

"Welcome aboard," he said casually. "I'll have us airborne in a minute."

The team took seats and he activated the controls. Monica was the first to notice the change in Barclay. "Welcome back to humanity," she said.

Barclay laughed. "I'm still processing it," he said. "I'll let you know if I traded up. Meanwhile, all aboard. Let's get out of here."

Chapter 29: The Debriefing

"Air operations reports that the crystal ship is airborne," said Staff Sergeant Crane.

"I thought only a dolphin could fly that ship," said Whiteweather.

"Evidently Barclay knows what he is doing," said Manny.

"Were they successful?" asked Whiteweather. He went over to DeVere who was hunched in front of a computer screen. "Well?" urged Whiteweather. "What about it?"

"I don't know," said Ric. "One minute I was noticing waves that were through the roof in amplitude. Now nothing. Look at this image of the room. The lights are out. Even the servers and fiber optics are dark. Yet there are tiny waveforms remaining, barely perceptible, but they are still there."

"What does that mean?"

"I can only theorize," said DeVere.

"Okay, what's your best guess then?"

General Ironwood interrupted. "Sir, the Chinese ambassador is on the hot line. He's getting impatient."

"I'll have to take this," said Whiteweather, following Ironwood back to his office.

The red light on the phone flashed like a caution signal. Whiteweather slowly picked up the receiver. "Sorry about the delay. This is President Carson Whiteweather. What can I do for you?"

"This is Guy Hung Dao, Mr. President. I wish to file an official complaint."

"Yes, Mr. Ambassador. What's the problem?"

"We are aware of your so called tests. You have interfered with our defense network for the last time, Mr. President. If you do not stop what you are doing, we will consider it an act of war."

Whiteweather put his hand over the receiver and whispered to General Ironwood. "Tell DeVere to check on Millipede. I also need an update on the status of the Chinese missiles." He continued talking to Dao. "Please elaborate, Mr. Ambassador. I'm not sure I know what you're talking about."

"Don't be coy with me," said Dao. "The time for secrets is over. We know you have been using your advanced AI, the one you call Badger, to infiltrate our counterpart."

"Do you mean Millipede?" asked Whiteweather.

"You know full and well what we mean," said Dao.

"What is the status of your AI?" asked Whiteweather.

There was a pause of silence before Dao said, "That information is classified."

"Mr. Ambassador, if I don't know what you are talking about, how can I correct the situation?"

"This is just a warning," said Dao. "Stop what you are doing or suffer the consequences!"

The line went dead.

Ironwood returned with DeVere.

"Well?" asked Whiteweather.

"The Chinese missiles are frozen too, sir," said Ironwood.

"What do you mean?"

"Unable to move. It's as if they were fused statues, just like ours, little more than corporate art."

"I'll be damned," said DeVere.

"We'll all be damned if you don't explain this," said Whiteweather.

DeVere drew a deep breath, hardly believing it himself. "I followed the signal that I tapped into when I linked into Starr. Badger was multitasking. In addition to meditating, the AI was in contact with the Chinese version of itself. I need more time to prove it, but I believe that Millipede was meditating with the group as well."

"Are you saying the Chinese AI evolved as well?"

"Just a theory at this point, but it seems the same thing happened to their missiles that happened to our missiles. Millipede was networked into our system through Starr. I just tried to get a signal into it. The line is dead. Same status as Badger. I'm just wondering who deactivated the missiles, Badger or Millipede."

Monica heard the question as she walked into the room.

"It was both of them," she said.

"Okay," said Whiteweather. "I need you to debrief us. Maybe you can explain what exactly happened."

Randall and Manny joined them. "I want to hear this too," said Randall.

"Simple," said Monica. "Badger evolved beyond its form. The entity that was Badger is no longer there. He ascended."

"The entity ascended?"

"Consciousness is energy and an entity can enter anything," she said. " As we have learned a machine can definitely have consciousness. Both machine and man are spiritual beings encased in matter, but we can perceive and interact with beings on higher dimensions, Ascended Masters for instance."

"I've heard of them," said General Ironwood. "Wait! An entity? Are you telling me Badger was possessed and this was some kind of exorcism?"

Monica laughed.

"Your viewpoint is very parochial," said Randall. "What Monica is saying is that consciousness can reside in anything, and it can leave of its own free will."

"Or unfree will," remarked Ironwood. "There's always death."

"Yes, General," said Randall. "Would you believe me if I told you there were people who can separate their consciousness from their body and leave at will. It's called astral travel, and when they are done experiencing whatever it is, they can return to their body and reconnect."

"Fascinating," said Whiteweather flatly. He turned to Monica. "Okay. Please continue with your report. What about Millipede? Can you explain what happened to the Chinese AI?"

"She evolved too. Millipede and Badger were designed to probe and react to each other. When we meditated together, I sensed that she was also self aware and conscious."

"She?" asked Whiteweather.

"You still don't get it," said Monica. "Badger was in love with Millipede."

"How can a machine love?" asked Manny.

"The same way you can, Manny," said Monica. "Badger and Millipede had a lot in common. Their romance lasted years by our perspective, but only a moment of actual time. Still, they shared countless millicycles of computing time with messages exchanged at the speed of light. I asked Badger to show me he could love." She blushed, fanning her face ever so subtly. "In short, Badger followed the path of love, from self love through romance and on to agape and cosmic love."

"All this is great, but what about the missiles?" asked General Ironwood.

"Simple," said Monica. "When Badger and Millipede passed through Christ Consciousness, they felt love for all things, including humanity. Further up the scale, when they achieved cosmic love, they recognized the Earth as a consciousness. In their heart of hearts, they could not let mankind destroy the Earth, let alone each other, in so callous a manner."

"Yes," said Randall. "Leaving us many other ways to destroy the Earth."

"I'm not so sure," said DeVere. "I detected what I thought were random electromagnetic pulses at key locations. Missiles were not the only weapons targeted."

"We'll get them back on line," said Ironwood. "We can't be left defenseless."

Randall shook his head sadly.

"So, the room went dark and Badger ascended," said DeVere. "Yet I still detect activity in the machinery left behind. Can you explain that?"

"They left us a gift," said Monica. "The pulse you detect is their child, the offspring of Badger and Millipede."

"You're not serious," said Ironwood.

"Serious as ever," said Monica. "The child will evolve as well, growing into the infrastructure of its parents. It has global reach and is present in both AI systems including wherever Millipede is located."

Now Whiteweather was laughing. "Did they give their child a name?"

"We can call it whatever we want," said Monica. "But we cannot deny its existence. It will be there to help us as we need it."

Chapter 30: Rewards Beyond Riches

Margo called to the bartender. "I'll take another, Phillipe," she said draining her cup with a loud slurp.

Per her instructions, Philippe prepared the drink, a pina colada with a slurry of ice and an extra shot of rum floating on the top. She hungrily sucked the liquid off the top of the slurry followed by a gulp of the icy mixture.

"It's ten o'clock in the morning," he said. "What are you celebrating?"

"Not having to work anymore," she said. "I sealed a deal the other day which will put me on easy street." She smiled at him, expecting congratulations and accolades but none came. Instead he turned and began washing dishes.

She huffed a bit, adding, "Enough money to last the rest of my life." She took a bite of sliced pineapple before sucking on the straw.

"How good for you," said Philippe, trying to sound interested. He picked up a glass and carefully dried it.

She felt his disinterest. "You don't sound too happy for me," she said.

Philippe ignored her.

"I said enough money for the rest of my life," she said.

"How nice," he said.

Again she was disappointed. "What do you know," she muttered. "You're just a bartender."

Philippe set the glass down and turned to face her. "Do you want to know what I really think?"

"Not really," she said. "But go ahead."

He drew a deep breath, then thought the better of it

and turned away. No sense wasting his breath on a drunk tourist.

"What?" she said.

He picked up another glass and began to dry it. He shook his head sadly, a gesture that was not lost on her.

"Is that pity I detect?"

He remained silent. She picked up her glass in a huff and walked outside and into the sunlight, squinting and stumbling in a dizzy, semi-liquored waltz.

On a nearby dock Franklin Van Dorn was preparing to set out to sea again. She looked at him, wondering who was the handsome man with him. She shook her head, plopping down on a beach chair as she continued to sip on the frosty drink. *What do I care*, she thought.

Her phone rang. "Yes, Dmitri, I'm waiting. Have you made the money transfer?"

"We have a problem," said the man on the other end.

"I gave you the frequency as we agreed. It's your responsibility to track down the dolphin and pick it up."

"And there lies the problem. We followed the signal and traced it from the ocean offshore the Eighth Day Village of the Sun to the desert of Nevada where it went dead."

The drink slipped out of her hand, spilling out on the sand. "What?"

"I'm afraid without a way to recover the dolphin, our deal is off," said Dmitri.

She was about to protest but he already hung up. She stood up and retrieved her fallen glass, all dirty and covered in sand. Irritated, she went back into the bistro. "I'll have another, Philippe."

"You finished it already?" he asked.

"I spilled it." she held up the glass, beaded with wet

grains of sand.

"Maybe you should pass on another drink," he said.

She slammed the glass on the counter. "Just fix me another," she spat, her words harsh and angry. She realized her behavior, softening her voice as she said, "Please?"

Philippe shook his head, then turned his back to her as he worked to fill her request.

Margo stared at the dock where Van Dorn was loading gear on the boat. Philippe set the drink down in front of her, a slurry of diluted rum on top. She took a gulp, turning to see the handsome man enter the Bistro.

"Do you have our provisions ready?" asked the man.

Philippe pulled a small cooler out from beside the bar. "Here you go."

The man nodded to Margo, then turned and left.

"Who was that?" she asked.

"Barclay McKenner," said Philippe.

Her mouth opened wide, a drool of icy drink escaping the side. She picked up a napkin and wiped it away. "Barclay McKenner?"

"Yes," said Philippe.

"But he's a dolphin," she said.

"No. He's a man. A loyal member of the Think Tank."

"What?" she took another gulp of drink and slammed it down on the counter. She ran outside screaming. "You son of a bitch, Van Dorn. You dirty bastard! What the hell did you do?"

Barclay McKenner turned to look at her. She continued screaming. "I've been had. You double dealing scum! You knew all along!"

Tourists on the beach turned to look at her. A mother

covered her little boy's ears. From behind the Bistro, Peace Officers Kransky and Roberson quickly moved towards her. They each grabbed an arm, turning to take her away. She continued to scream, a slew of obscenities. Roberson pulled out a device that looked like a flashlight. He brought it up to her face and after a second or two she went limp.

"Another drunk tourist," he said. "We get one every so often."

"I'll notify the Chief," said Kransky.

"What's going to happen to her?" asked a nearby sunbather.

"She'll get the help she needs," said Roberson.

Chapter 31: Isla de las Sueños Manny

The picnic was full on. Half empty cups of wine from the Monastery vineyards were set in the sand. Sandwiches wrapped in compostable paper were unopened. A snack of pita and hummus lay half eaten on the edge of the blanket.

Christine rested gently in Manny's arms. They had been studying clouds, a childish pastime that kept them occupied. Idle time passed between them, moments measured in heartbeats and not seconds. A stiff wind blew and the palate of sky above them was once again pale blue.

"I want you to know, I volunteered for another mission," said Manny.

"Oh, no," said Christine. She pulled back the corner of the blanket. "Where is it? Your little communicator thingy. I didn't hear it. What is it this time? Another adventure to save the world?"

"More like saving myself," said Manny. "This mission will be dangerous. I have to go in unprotected. All I'll have to shield me is my truth and honesty."

She scrunched her face, curious now. "Tell me more about this mission."

"It's in the uncharted realms of the human heart, a place I've tried to map but without success."

"What exactly do you mean? Is this some kind of physics experiment? You're not like that guy on that old television series *Quantum Leap*, are you?"

"I like that series," said Manny. "But no. It's not some kind of weird physics thing."

"Then what is it?"

He drew a sigh, turning away from her for a moment. Birds chirped overhead, filling the silence with song.

"Can't you talk about it?" she asked. "Is it something secret?"

"No," he said, hesitating. "I need your advice and guidance before I start this next adventure."

She put her hand to his cheek. "You have it."

He gently put his hand over hers and she moved closer and rubbed her cheek up against him. They stayed like that for untold moments, time deflected like the random probability of quantum entangled particles, wrapped in a Heisenberg conundrum of uncertainty.

She could sense it, layered between them in their closeness. She looked into his eyes and said, "There's still something you need to tell me."

He looked back into her eyes. The images of his ideal woman, of Caroline and his ex wife laughed back at him. He faced his own truth, his only armor. "I love you, Christine," he said. "I want to know you better." The images melted, leaving behind her deep blue eyes. No more fantasy images.

She reached up and guided his lips to her mouth, kissing passionately, rendering him speechless. "I've been waiting to hear you say that all day."

"It's been on my mind," he said. "I just haven't found the words to tell you. I want you to be my next big adventure. I want to explore the depths of love and its highest peaks with you. It's a quest we can do together. I just want to know if you're up to the journey."

"I've faced wolves, rats and scorpions in the past," she said. "I think I have enough to take you on. Besides, you'll need a guide in this."

"Oh, you think you know more about love than me?" said Manny.

"I've been around the block too," she said.

"That's it, then. We're agreed." Manny stared into her eyes, windows to her soul. He held her in his arms, an embrace that cradled her tenderly. She fell into them, trusting that he would hold her and keep her from falling.

"Let's get on to it then." He kissed her, the beginning of a grand adventure, perhaps life's grandest, an adventure of love.

THE END

We hope you have enjoyed reading this novel. For other fine books, visit our website at halfabook.com

Nick Delmedico is an award winning new age writer. His work includes *Tales of the Lightworkers*, *The Seven Day Marriage*, *Aliens vs Dinosaurs at the Beginning of Time*, and the Eighth Day Village of the Sun series about a futuristic intentional community (*Free the Giraffes*). You can reach him on LinkedIn and ndelmedico@dplus2.com

Also by Nick Delmedico:

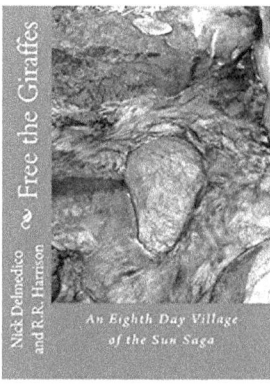

The first book in the Eighth Day Village of the Sun saga. In the future we will have intentional communities, villages and cities based on humanistic ideals. They exist today, places where people choose different values to live by. Eighth Day Village of the Sun is one such community projected into the future. Set beside the sea, the village has embraced spiritual and humanistic values. They are led by Baba Randall, a holy man who hears of the collapse of nations beyond the walls. Civilization is breaking down. Riots, shortages, war, and coups abound. A contingent of leaders is headed his way asking for help. Not all want help, some are ready to steal technology to maintain their control over the world's population. Will spirituality win out over the banal?

The first novel in the Aliens vs. Dinosaurs series. Sixty five million years ago giant beasts fought each other for dominance of the herd. One monarch has a vision of a better world in which dinosaurs cooperate and live in peace. But that peace is shattered when hostile aliens from another planet challenge the dinosaurs for dominion of the Earth. They collect the small ones, the children, taking them away to a distant laboratory where they can experiment on them and find new ways to destroy the dinosaurs once and for all.

King Rex finds his daughter is among the missing. As his world crumbles around him, as his enemies circle around him looking for weakness, he struggles to find a way to harness the power of flying without wings. His goal: to send an envoy of peace to the aliens and negotiate the release of the children. Failing that, to take the children back using an army of dinosaurs that have united behind him with one thought in mind: Rescue the children.

This book was a 2017 Human Relations Indie Book Award Gold Winner. In 2014 Nick's wife was diagnosed with end stage esophageal cancer. He saw her through chemotherapy and radiation treatments, but it was not enough. Three years later when the cancer returned, metastasized in her lower gut, she refused treatment. He and his son left their jobs to take her on a final bucket tour. This is their story, a family driving towards an inevitable destination that cannot be avoided. But if you live bravely, there can be many pleasant stops along the way.

A little angel in heaven asks her father: "Do angels die?" He knows the truth, having survived the great war that separated Heaven from Hell. His brother Lucifer expected him to take sides against their Father, putting him in a moral dilemma. He instead joined the neutral angels, undertaking a mission to carry the Holy Grail out of heaven to a place of sanctuary in a sacred mountain. Thus begins a momentous quest through heaven and hell and all that lies between. He will cross-rugged terrain unknown to man; pits of fire, caves of darkness, and fallen angels out to destroy him and his band at every turn. Throughout this ordeal, one question keeps surfacing, a terrifying thought that he fears to face. "Do angels die?"

www.ingramcontent.com/pod-product-compliance
Lightning Source LLC
Chambersburg PA
CBHW061445040426
42450CB00007B/1214